Cambridge Opera Handbooks

Richard Wagner
Parsifal

Emil Scaria as Gurnemanz in Wagner's production of
Parsifal; Bayreuth, 1882

Richard Wagner
Parsifal

LUCY BECKETT

CAMBRIDGE UNIVERSITY PRESS

Cambridge
London   New York   New Rochelle
Melbourne   Sydney

Published by the Press Syndicate of the University of Cambridge
The Pitt Building, Trumpington Street, Cambridge CB2 1RP
32 East 57th Street, New York, NY 10022, USA
296 Beaconsfield Parade, Middle Park, Melbourne 3206, Australia

First published 1981

Printed and bound in Great Britain by
Redwood Burn Limited
Trowbridge and Esher

British Library Cataloguing in Publication Data

Beckett, Lucy
Richard Wagner, Parsifal. – (Cambridge opera handbooks).
1. Wagner, Richard. Parsifal
I. Title   II. Series
782.1'092'4   ML410.W17   80-40870
ISBN 0 521 22825 5 hard covers
ISBN 0 521 29662 5 paperback

General preface

This is a series of studies of individual operas, written for the serious opera-goer or record-collector as well as the student or scholar. Each volume has three main concerns. The first is historical: to describe the genesis of the work, its sources or its relation to literary prototypes, the collaboration between librettist and composer, and the first performance and subsequent stage history. This history is itself a record of changing attitudes towards the work, and an index of general changes of taste. The second is analytical and it is grounded in a very full synopsis which considers the opera as a structure of musical and dramatic effects. In most volumes there is also a musical analysis of a section of the score, showing how the music serves or makes the drama. The analysis, like the history, naturally raises questions of interpretation, and the third concern of each volume is to show how critical writing about an opera, like production and performance, can direct or distort appreciation of its structural elements. Some conflict of interpretation, is an inevitable part of this account; editors of the handbooks reflect this — by citing classic statements, by commissioning new essays, by taking up their own critical position. A final section gives a select bibliography, a discography and guides to other sources.

In working out plans for these volumes, the Cambridge University Press was responding to an initial stimulus from staff of the English National Opera. Particular thanks are due to Mr Edmund Tracey and Mr Nicholas John for help, advice and suggestions.

Books published

W. A. Mozart: *Don Giovanni* by Julian Rushton
C. W. von Gluck: *Orfeo* by Patricia Howard

Other volumes in preparation

to
Christopher Brett

Contents

Illustrations

Acknowledgements

The author would like to thank Mr Harold Rosenthal for the loan of material from his library for the stage history chapter and for the frontispiece, and the management of the Festspielhaus, Bayreuth, for permission to use copyright photographs for the other illustrations.

Ich muss mit diesem letzten Werke volle Freiheit haben; denn in Tell's Weise muss ich sagen: entrinnt auch dieses kraftlos meinen Händen, hab' ich kein weiteres mehr zu versenden.

With this last work I must have complete freedom; for like Tell I have to say: if even this falls powerless from my hands, I have no other to send after it.

Wagner to King Ludwig II, 25 August 1879

1 Wieland Wagner's set for Klingsor's castle, Act II Scene 1;
Bayreuth 1951—73, with some modifications

1   *The sources*

The quest [for sources] tends to operate in one direction only — away from the masterpiece. . .The effort to retrogress towards the source remains largely gratuitous if the procedure is not inverted and pressed forward to appreciate the point at which source and influence are subsumed in the final synthesis.

P. Mansell Jones, quoted in *Arthurian Literature in the Middle Ages,* ed. R. S. Loomis, p. 546

Wagner's *Parsifal* is, among many other things, a modern re-working of the legend of the Holy Grail, the mystical cup of the Last Supper in quest of which the Christian knight must journey through the tribulations of the world. English readers are familiar with the outlines of this legend from the late version of it given in Malory's *Morte Darthur* and reproduced with the muted melancholy of Victorian romanticism in Tennyson's *Idylls of the King.* It is important to realize at the outset that although Wagner's Grail is indeed the cup of the Last Supper, Wagner's principal source, the Middle High German poet Wolfram von Eschenbach, portrays the Grail as a magic stone without specifically Christian significance. Wolfram's own chief source, the twelfth-century French poet Chrétien de Troyes, has at the centre of his *Perceval* a magic dish which, equally, has no association with the Last Supper or with the cup in which Joseph of Arimathea caught the blood of Christ. The text of Chrétien's *Perceval* which Wagner eventually read, however, included later continuations in which the Grail had acquired its Christian history. The point of outlining this somewhat complicated genealogy of sources is to establish that Wagner's imagination was seized by a Grail legend full of striking scenes and dramatic encounters but with no eucharistic connotations, and that even when he found in Chrétien confirmation of his desire to give the Grail its Christian force he was in fact reading a later version of the tale than Wolfram's and not an earlier one.

Wagner first read Wolfram von Eschenbach's *Parzival* in the summer of 1845. He was staying at the time in Marienbad, on holiday from

1

Dresden. Three months earlier he had finished the orchestration of *Tannhäuser*, the first performance of which took place the following October. During his few weeks of relaxation in Marienbad he wrote the detailed prose sketch of *Lohengrin*, drafted a comedy on the Nuremberg guild of Mastersingers, and saw in Wolfram's epic the distant prospect of his last work, of which he was to write the text in 1877, thirty-two years later.

Gradually, and with many intervals during which his mind was full of other things, the vision took definite shape. In 1860 — almost half-way through those thirty-two years — Wagner wrote from Paris to Mathilde Wesendonk:

Parzival is again very much coming to life in me; all the time I see it more and more clearly; when one day it is all finally ripe in me, the bringing of this poem into the world will be for me an extreme pleasure. But between now and then a good few years may yet have to pass. . .I shall put it off as long as I can, and I concern myself with it only when it forces me to. But then this extraordinary process of generation does let me forget all my troubles.[1]

One cannot discuss the 'sources' of Wagner's works in the same way as one may describe, in the history of other operas, a play or a tale turned by a librettist into an operatic text which is then 'set' by a composer. Wagner conceived each of his works as, from the beginning, a created fusion of words and music; he was capable of maintaining the generative process within himself over decades of his life — *Parsifal* is the most extreme case — until the work was 'finally ripe'; meanwhile his own experience, his changing ideas, books that he read, and the writing of his other works, were brought to bear on the original idea, influencing its complete form in various ways. The process that gave *Parsifal* its eventual dramatic life, the evolution in Wagner's mind of this particular plot and set of characters, this particular imaginative world, is the subject of this chapter.

Wolfram von Eschenbach's *Parzival* is a chivalric romance of almost 25,000 lines of verse, written at the beginning of the thirteenth century. It tells, in the rambling and episodic manner characteristic of the period, the story of Parzival's knightly life, from his fatherless childhood in the forest, where his mother keeps him from the perilous world in ignorance, to his final triumph as Lord of the Grail. Wagner, a long while after he had read the poem, and from within the new realities constructed by his own imagination, was very scornful of Wolfram. As he wrote to Mathilde Wesendonk in 1859:

You see how easy Meister Wolfram made it for himself. Never mind that he understands nothing whatever of the real content; he strings incident to incident, adventure to adventure, makes the Grail the centre of odd and peculiar goings-on, blunders about, and leaves the serious reader wondering what he is really up to. . .Wolfram is a thoroughly raw phenomenon, for which his barbaric and muddled period must take the blame, slung as it was between ancient Christendom and the newer order of the secular state.[2]

But Wolfram's *Parzival* is the masterpiece of Middle High German poetry. For all its apparent discursiveness, there is a striking symmetry in its organization, and it reflects a world – that bounded by the conventions of Christian knighthood – in its way as orderly and civilized as any that came after it. What is more, it is clear from all that followed in the development of his own *Parsifal* that Wagner responded strongly not only to the poem's surface, the lively dialogue and glittering description, but also to its substance. For substance Wolfram expresses and understands, even if Wagner later wanted to believe that all the substance was in his own interpretation of a legend naively presented by the poor confused medieval poet.

The real subject of Wolfram's poem is the contrast between constancy and inconstancy, faithfulness and uncertainty, truth and wavering, or however one chooses to translate 'triuwe' and 'zwivel' ('Treue' and 'Zweifel' in the modern German in which Wagner read the poem). The poem opens; 'If inconstancy is the heart's neighbour, the soul will not fail to find it bitter.'[3] And in the long course of the story the ignorant boy has to learn faithfulness to something – the Grail – which at first sight he has understood not at all, and which he then has to find again through the faithfulness he has learnt. Three short quotations will give some idea of the atmosphere with which Wolfram surrounds Parzival's quest.

When the hideous messenger of the Grail, the Loathly Damsel of the English Arthurian tales, curses Parzival for his careless silence in the castle of the Grail, Parzival is stricken:

I cannot cast off my sorrow. . .I can find no words for my suffering as I feel it within me when many a one, not understanding my grief, torments me, and I must then endure his scorn as well. I will allow myself no joy until I have seen the Grail, be the time short or long. My thoughts drive me toward that goal, and never will I swerve from it as long as I shall live.[4]

Several times, later in the poem, he leaves some scene of victory or comfort unrecognized in his armour as he travels on, his lonely departures conveying, through many adventures, the melancholy of his quest. On one of these occasions Wolfram says: 'They thanked him and begged him to stay with them. But the goal he had set lay far away, and the good knight turned his course to where great ease was rare; strife was all he sought. In the times when he lived no man, I think, ever fought so much as he.' [5]

At the conclusion of the whole poem Wolfram sums up Parzival's fidelity: 'A life so ended that God is not robbed of the soul through guilt of love, and which can obtain the favour of the world with honour, that is a worthy work.' [6]

Here was a poet who kept the real content of his story firmly in view, whatever the picturesque sprawl of his narrative. And here was a hero truly after the heart of the composer who had already written *Der fliegende Holländer* and *Tannhäuser,* who hankered obsessively for the purity of renunciation, and who all his life not only pursued with fierce resolution the goals he had set himself but watched himself doing so with pride. It is clear that the steadfast and tormented wandering at last expressed by the sixty-five-year-old composer in the prelude to the third act of *Parsifal* had been, whatever his intervening denials, the deeply sympathetic theme which had seized the imagination of the young man of thirty-two.

There were also, of course, more straightforward debts to Wolfram. Wagner's *Parsifal* – he eventually adopted this spelling, just as he changed Wolfram's Anfortas to Amfortas – has four characters of intense counter-balancing individuality: Parsifal, the naive hero who through compassion comes to understanding; Amfortas, the guilty and suffering king, unwilling lord of the Grail; Klingsor, the evil enemy of the Grail who has corrupted Amfortas; and Kundry, the woman torn by complex psychological strife in whom the destinies of the other three meet and are resolved. Gurnemanz, though his role is the longest in the work, will, as a character outside the intense emotional geometry connecting these four, be considered later.

In Wolfram's *Parzival* only the hero himself is a rounded character seen from the inside, and allowed to develop and change under the pressure of experience; indeed, as we have seen, this development is the central theme of the poem, which might well be called the archetypal *Bildungsroman.* The character of Parsifal Wagner took from Wolfram without essential modification. The poet's several dozen other characters are two-dimensional and without growth; even the knight Gawan, whose adventures form a long digression from, and foil to, the history of Parzival, is unaltered by the ordeals from which he emerges with unfailing bravado. As for Anfortas, we see his pain and – on Parzival's victorious return to the Grail – his cure. We are not made to feel that he suffers also from guilt, and we are told only in the most sketchy and external fashion of how he came to grief. He is not a character in the dramatic sense, but a mere figure in the legendary machinery through which Parzival arrives at his triumph. Nevertheless, Wolfram provides the material of Wagner's Amfortas. For example, Wolfram presents the vivid surface detail of the confrontation, full of irony and latent significance, between Parzival and Anfortas, in a word the *scene* from which Wagner could build his character outwards and backwards. Examination of this scene in Wolfram suggests, indeed, that here was the primary spark which fired Wagner's dramatic imagination.

Parzival, brash, impulsive and innocent, blunders into the luxurious splendour of the castle of the Grail.

The lord of the castle was brought into the hall and placed as he bade, on a couch facing the central fireplace. He had paid his debt to joy; his life was but a dying. Into the great hall came the radiant Parzival. . .The sorrowful host, because of his illness, kept blazing fires and wore warm clothing. The coat of fur and the cloak over it were lined outside and in with sable skins wide and long.[7]

When Wagner first read this, his Wotan and Siegfried, his Sachs and Walther, were all in the future. But the dramatic contrast between an old man laden with knowledge and grief and the careless, ignorant young man who is to be his heir clearly had for him some deep emotional appeal. It is a strong theme of all his mature works, and in *Parsifal,* for which he eventually devised a plot in which the young man must undergo the very same experience as the old, it reached its purest form. This plot is not in Wolfram. For the moment the point is only that in this scene, where the foolish boy sees the wounded king languishing in the castle hall and understands nothing of what he sees, Wagner found the germ of his drama. When he came at last to write it he reproduced Wolfram's scene exactly, and one may even say that the rest of his work is a psychological extrapolation from it.

Wagner's eye for a scene, a telling stage-picture in which characters are suspended in significance like flies in amber, is fundamental to his genius as a dramatist. For years he saw Siegfried, the dead hero, carried from the stage; and from the picture grew the whole of the *Ring.* For years he saw Wolfram's hall of the Grail, the wounded king, the silent, clumsy boy, and from the picture invented the story which binds the two characters together. There is a second scene in Wolfram's *Parzival* which obviously struck him with almost equal force: the knight concealed in his armour who arrives alone in a forest clearing and is asked by a grey old man why he is bearing arms on Good Friday. This scene also is reproduced in the opera, its emotional essentials expanded but not changed. Between what became Act I Scene 2 and Act III Scene 1 of Wagner's *Parsifal*, between the ignorant youth of the Grail hall and the weary knight of Good Friday morning, there had to lie Act II, the transformation of the one into the other. To dramatize this transformation Wagner fused into one remarkable encounter several disparate episodes and characters in Wolfram and other versions of the Grail legend.

In a notebook of 1854, where Parzival is mentioned for the first time since the Marienbad holiday of 1845, the pilgrim knight puts in a brief appearance in the third act of a preliminary sketch for *Tristan*. In *Mein Leben* Wagner said of this soon abandoned plan: 'The picture of Tristan languishing, yet unable to die of his wound, identified itself in my mind with Anfortas in the Romance of the Grail.'[8] At this point Parsifal and Amfortas, in their relation of healer and sufferer, are the still active residue of the first reading of Wolfram, gathering significance from the now powerful influence of Schopenhauer. 'Parzival's Refrain = the whole world nothing but unsatisfied yearning', says the notebook entry.[9]

Three years later, the peace of a spring morning in his little house at the bottom of Mathilde Wesendonk's garden reminded Wagner of the second essential Wolfram scene, the homecoming of the pilgrim knight, and he dashed off a sketch for a three-act *Parsifal* drama which has not survived. Houston Stewart Chamberlain in his 'Notes sur *Parsifal*' in the *Revue wagnérienne* of August 1886 says that his sketch contained important scenes to be found in the finished work and also fragments of musical motives. Whether he had actually seen the sketch himself is not clear. A fragment of music written down for Mathilde Wesendonk the following year (1858) and reckoned to be the 'Parzival's Refrain' of the *Tristan* note-book, contains a faint foreshadowing of the eventual Grail theme, and a few words expressing the longing of the traveller who must journey from his first vain encounter with the Grail to its ultimate re-discovery:

> Wo find ich dich, du heil'ger Gral
> dich sucht voll Sehnsucht mein Herze.[10]

> Where shall I find you, Holy Grail,
> full of longing my heart seeks you.

Shortly after sending this note to Frau Wesendonk, Wagner was forced to leave Zurich by the explosion of his complicated domestic situation. In the following two years — summer 1858 to summer 1860 —

in Venice, Lucerne, and finally Paris, he composed *Tristan* and nursed the conception of *Parsifal*. The connection between the two was above all his constant reading of Schopenhauer. In his commentary on this period (his diary for Mathilde Wesendonk and long letters to her) can be traced the progress of his *Parsifal* from its two seminal scenes to almost complete dramatic shape.

By the autumn of 1858 Parsifal's journey from innocence to wisdom is becoming involved, in Wagner's mind, with Schopenhauer's philosophy of pity as the learning and transcendence of suffering. Paraphrasing Schopenhauer, Wagner in his diary contrasts compassion (*Mitleid*) with love, the will to live at its most acute. Whereas love (*Mitfreude*) fastens upon the individual, the particular, and, when raised to its height, is most extremely a matter of the self and the single other (the theme of *Tristan*), compassion is general and undifferentiated and may be extended to the whole of creation. It has to do with learning: 'the point here is not what another suffers, but what I suffer if I understand his suffering. We know what exists outside us only in so far as we can imagine it for ourselves, and as I imagine it for myself, so it exists for me.' At the same time compassion has to do with salvation. 'If the suffering [of animals] can have an object, it is only through the awakening of pity in man, who takes upon himself the flawed existence of the animals and becomes the liberator of the world, above all by recognizing the error of all existence. (One day, in the third act of *Parsifal*, the meaning of all this will become clear to you.)'[11] The place of animals in the argument was important to Wagner and is not irrelevant to *Parsifal*, as we shall see.

In Wolfram's poem, Parzival, on his first visit to the castle of the Grail, fails only to ask Anfortas a simple question that will heal his wound. In all this theorizing on the quasi-religious and epistemological significance of compassion, Wagner, with the help of Schopenhauer, is deepening and making more subtle the relation between his two central characters. The dramatizing of this relation — the filling of the gap between the first great scene and the second with a single convulsion of plot and character — remains a nebulous problem. One hint of its solution is given in a letter of December 1858: '*Parzival* has much occupied me: in particular an idea for a singular creation has come to me, a marvellous woman, a demonic force (the messenger of the Grail), who grows more and more alive and striking.'[12] But in the next long discussion of the slowly evolving *Parsifal* idea, in May 1859, this woman is not mentioned. Parsifal and Amfortas alone are still preoccupying Wagner. He has re-read Wolfram (this is the letter in which he speaks so contemptuously of his principal source) and explored other Grail legends. The project now seems beset with difficulties. The Grail, in Wolfram a mere magic stone fallen from the sky, must be given the weight of the stories which make it the chalice of the Last Supper and the vessel in which Joseph of Arimathea caught the blood of Christ on the cross. This will raise the suffering of Amfortas to a quite different level and give to his guardianship, his wound and his inability to die a moral and religious value of which Wolfram had no conception: 'my Tristan of the third act,' as Wagner says, 'with an inconceivable increase'. At the same time the 'flat and meaningless matter of the question' in Wolfram is only one of the difficulties surrounding the character of Parsifal. 'If Amfortas is to be set in the true light due to him, he acquires such powerful tragic force that it is practically impossible to set a second major character over against him, yet Parsifal must carry the interest of a major character if he is not to arrive at the end as a coldly resolving *deus ex machina.* So that Parsifal's development. . .must be brought back to the foreground.' Here Wagner reaches the nub of his problem. 'And for this I have no option, no broad scheme such as Wolfram could command; I must so compress it all into three main situations of drastic substance that the profound, ramifying meaning is presented clearly and distinctly; for *thus* to work and put across material is, after all, *my* art.'[13]

The second act was the crux, and a third major character the instrument by which Parsifal and Amfortas should be kept in balance and the philosophical content, the learning of and redemption through pity, compelled into dramatic form. By August 1860 Wagner had found his solution. 'Have I told you before that the fabulous wild messenger of the Grail is to be one and the same being as the seductive woman of the second act? Since this struck me, almost all my material has become clear to me.' There follows a long, detailed description of Kundry as she was indeed to appear in the finished work. She is to be the mysterious, haggard servant of the Grail, cowering in corners yet scornful of the knights,

her eye apparently always seeking the right one. . .but she does not know what she seeks: it is only instinct. When the stupid Parsifal arrives she can't take her eyes off him. . .She is in a state of unspeakable agitation and anxiety. . .Does she hope – to be able to reach an end? What does she hope from Parsifal? Surely she fastens on him some unheard-of claim? But it's all shadowy and dark: no knowledge, only stress, twilight. . .Now can you guess who the marvellous bewitching woman is, whom Parsifal finds in the mysterious castle?[14]

The excitement of these paragraphs is understandable. Wagner has found his connecting character, by means of whom Parsifal is to be linked to Amfortas by identical experience; and in finding his character he has solved the problem of his plot and its dramatic presentation. Kundry, who has been the agent of Amfortas's fall, will be the instrument of Parsifal's triumph, whereby both Amfortas and she herself will be saved. Parsifal (and the audience) will learn from her the meaning of Amfortas's wound; they will also learn of Parsifal's own past cruelty, in carelessly deserting his mother for the glamour of the knightly life, for the consequence of Kundry's magic ubiquity is deep knowledge. She passes, in a condition of cataleptic trance, from her existence as the haunted, driven servant of the Grail to her role as seductive temptress (though here too haunted and driven) corrupting the knights of the Grail from their chaste guardianship. From her own despair she can be rescued only by one who resists her: thus, as a character in her own right and no mere agent, she has sunk still further into misery through Amfortas's fall, and will be saved for ever by Parsifal's victory over her.

This extraordinary woman, certainly the strangest and perhaps the most profound of all Wagner's characters, is the result of creative meditation at who knows what conscious or unconscious levels of his mind. It is possible, however, to trace some of the elements which fused to produce her, and to show how they came together to meet what Wagner felt to be the underlying psychological requirements of the relationship between Parsifal and Amfortas, as well as the simple dramatic needs of his second act.

In Wolfram's poem, Kundry is the Loathly Damsel of other Arthurian tales. Hideous and deformed, but endowed with magic powers and great learning, she appears at Arthur's court to curse Parzival for his hard-hearted silence at the castle of the Grail. Much later, after all Parzival's faithful wandering, she reappears with the news that words magically written round the Grail have revealed Parzival as its new lord, who will return to heal Anfortas by his question. On this occasion, most strikingly, she is full of sorrow and contrition and weeps before Parzival, begging his forgiveness. The reason for her shame is obscure, since even if she had been wrong to curse Parzival earlier, it was her curse which first showed him that he must seek the Grail again, and which successfully tested his fidelity through his travels. In any case Parzival 'lost his anger toward her and forgave her, but without a kiss.'[15] This is all that Wolfram tells us of 'Cundrie la sorcière'. She is a messenger of sinister aspect whose news is of the Grail and scarcely at all of Parzival's soul. Several other characters in Wolfram's poem, however, contribute something to Wagner's Kundry. Parzival meets his cousin Sigune, a sad maiden mourning the death of her love, four times in the course of the poem. The first time she tells him his name, by which his mother had never called him; the second time she reproaches him for his failure at the castle of the Grail; the third time she is a penitent hermit whom at first he does not recognize: she recognizes him only when he takes off his helmet; the fourth time she is dead. All of these encounters are reproduced by Wagner in the relationship between his Kundry and his Parsifal.

The news that he has caused his mother's death from grief by deserting her — the news that Wagner's Kundry gives him in such a way as to prepare his emotions for her own assault upon them — comes to Wolfram's Parzival from Trevrizent, an old knight retired alone to the forest. Immediately afterwards Trevrizent tells Parzival the whole story of Anfortas's wound and how he may not die because the Grail keeps him alive, and may not be cured until he is asked the magic question. Parzival's guilt at his mother's death is therefore instantly compounded and confused with his guilt at having failed Anfortas.

Wagner's Kundry as teacher, bringer of news (*Kunde*), has in her something of Wolfram's Cundrie, Sigune and Trevrizent. As a woman of compelling sexual power she has qualities drawn from other characters in the poem. Wolfram's Parzival, in this at his furthest distance from Wagner's hero, wins himself a wife early in the story and has almost at once to leave her. In the nineteenth-century translations, her name is spelt Kundwiramur. Parzival's longing to return to her is throughout the tale bound up with his quest for the Grail, and his faithfulness to her leads him to avoid all other courtly entanglements. But for all her beauty his first night with her is passed in chaste innocence, and something of the atmosphere of this scene Wagner retains in Parsifal's encounter with Kundry. In contrast to Parzival's demure wife, Wolfram's poem also contains an untameable seductress, the Lady Orgeluse, who, after the conquest of many knights, at last yields to the dashing Gawan whom she taunts with Kundry-like devilment. Parzival himself, anonymous in his armour, coldly rejects her, and, very late in the poem, we are told that she is the lady responsible for Anfortas's downfall. Wolfram sets no high value on absolute chastity, nor does he associate with it the guardianship of the Grail. The tale of Anfortas's wounding is lightly told and Orgeluse herself is a peripheral character in the story of Parzival. Nevertheless, as with all these components of Wagner's Kundry, the surface detail suggested to the composer depths quite remote from the world of the medieval poet. The knight who wounded Anfortas was a heathen who longed to win the Grail and had its name engraved on his spear, perhaps the same spear which is carried with a drop of blood at its tip (in Wolfram) in procession before the Grail. Furthermore, Orgeluse, when Gawan wins her, is in the power of a sorceror named Clinschor who holds enchanted in his *Schastel merveil* four queens and four hundred maidens. 'All the bright flowers blooming there were as nothing to the radiance of Orgeluse. . . That was Clinschor's forest.'[16] Gawan releases the defeated Clinschor's captives and is afterwards told of Clinschor's earlier castration at the hands of a cuckolded king of Sicily.

From this plethora of characters and incidents Wagner formed not only his Kundry, his single woman who should connect the fallen, guilty Amfortas with the innocent, victorious Parsifal, but also his Klingsor, the self-castrated magician who, possessed with destructive envy of the Grail, uses Kundry to seduce its guardian knights and holds his victims spellbound in his castle. Klingsor has in common with Alberich the renunciation of love for power, and represents the forces of darkness in a fairly straightforward manner. The manifold sources of the complex Kundry, however, are not accounted for even in the several Wolfram characters who variously pre-figure her (she even shares with Wolfram's heathen Feirefiz the baptism which enables her to approach the Grail in Wagner's last scene).

In 1848 Wagner had sketched a scenario for a play called *Jesus of Nazareth*. The project came to nothing. But in one scene Wagner had Mary Magdalen kneeling in repentance at Jesus's feet on the shore of Lake Gennesareth and saying that she wished only to serve his followers as their humblest slave; later in the play she was to anoint his head and wash his feet. It should be emphasized that Parsifal and Kundry never, in Wagner's mind, represented Christ and the Magdalen: he was annoyed by suggestions (Wolzogen's, for example, in 1878) that this was so. Nevertheless, the scene, the stage-picture, stayed with him, and the penitent Magdalen is certainly one more of Kundry's forebears.

A scheme to which Wagner gave more prolonged consideration, and which had much closer links with *Parsifal,* was his plan for a Buddhist drama, *Die Sieger.* This was conceived and sketched in 1856, under the strong sway of Schopenhauer's writings. Schopenhauer saw in Christianity, Buddhism and Brahmanism a shared denial of the will to live, a shared ideal of ascetic renunciation, which proved to him their common source. He regarded the churches' dilution of this doctrine as a perverse accommodation to Judaism, and held to a view of final redemption as possible only through complete abnegation of the self. Chastity as the supremely powerful saving force reaches Wagner's *Parsifal* by way of these ideas: in *Die Sieger* its attainment was to have been the sole motive. (This was a revolution in Wagner's thought. In the notes accompanying the *Jesus of Nazareth* sketch he had condemned the ideal of chastity as 'the most complete and irremediable egoism' which 'lies at bottom of the monk's renunciation'.)[17] The plot of *Die Sieger* concerns a chaste young man, Ananda, who receives into the Brahmin community a beautiful girl, Prakriti, who has passionately loved him but is persuaded by the Buddha to renounce him. The Buddha reveals that in a previous incarnation Prakriti had rejected, with mocking laughter, the love of a Brahmin's son.

Here we have one of the deepest roots of the strange growth that was to be Kundry. Not only does she move from one existence to another under Klingsor's magic power; she has existed down the ages in one incarnation after another, and mocking laughter has been the cause of her anguished immortality. In the same letter in which Wagner describes her in such vivid detail, he says: 'Only thoughtful acceptance of the idea of transmigration of souls has been able to show me the consoling point at which all in the end converge at an equal height of redemption, after their differing paths through life, which in Time have run divided alongside one another, but which outside Time come together in full understanding.'[18] Kundry in the opera has been Gundryggia, a wandering spirit of Nordic mythology; she has also been Herodias who procured the death of John the Baptist, and a female version of Ahasuerus who laughed in the face of Christ and became the Wandering Jew, sharing with the Flying Dutchman an inability to escape in death a cursed existence. Parsifal's resistance to her breaks the curse and at last allows her to die, so that she may attain the Buddhist redemption of annihilation. Schopenhauer himself called *Schadenfreude* – Kundry's crime – 'the worst trait in human nature. . .It is diabolical and its derision is the laughter of hell.' It is, of course, the exact opposite of compassion. Schopenhauer also described the converging paths of Kundry and Parsifal (or Prakriti and Ananda) when he wrote of 'conversion of the will brought about by the suffering of life', and contrasted it with 'the other way, the narrow path of the elect, which leads to the same goal by means of mere knowledge and the consequent appropriation of the suffering of a whole world'.

The plan for *Die Sieger* progressed no further than the 1856 sketch, although in 1865 Wagner told King Ludwig that he was still intending to complete it before *Parsifal*. The sketch shows little promise of conflict and tension; Wagner himself realized that the bland, controlling figure of the Buddha was going to be difficult to transform into a dramatic character; most of all, the common motivation of *Die Sieger* and *Parsifal* meant that the idea of the Buddhist drama faded away as soon as *Parsifal* began to reach its final form. 'Since undertaking *Parsifal*,' Wagner wrote in 1882, 'I entirely abandoned the Buddhist project (related in a weaker sense to *Parsifal*), and I have never since then had it in mind to do anything with it.'[19]

With the invention − if a single word may be used to describe so multifarious a process − of Kundry, by the August of 1860, Wagner's scheme for *Parsifal* was almost complete in his mind. There he left it for several years more, knowing, as he said to Weissheimer in 1862 and to Mathilde Maier in 1864, that it was to be his last work.

Even for Wagner, who for most of his life picked himself up from one crisis only to greet the next, the summer of 1865 was a period of exceptional turmoil. In June Bülow had conducted the triumphant first performance of *Tristan* in Munich. In July Schnorr von Carolsfeld, Wagner's devoted first Tristan, suddenly died. Throughout August domestic and financial strain increased to an almost intolerable level: Wagner's accumulation of debts in Munich was making him extremely unpopular and worsening his already bad relations with King Ludwig's ministers. Although Wagner's first child had been born to Cosima von Bülow in April, she was still living with her husband and no resolution of this agonizing emotional tangle seemed in sight. Meanwhile Act II of *Siegfried* was half-scored and *Die Meistersinger* was half-composed. In the middle of all this Ludwig wrote asking to be told of Wagner's plans for *Die Sieger* and *Parsifal*. Wagner received the letter on 26 August. The following day he began to write out a prose sketch for *Parsifal*, finishing it three days later on 30 August. For those four days he escaped from the problems of real life into a created world which his imagination had already been assembling for twenty years. The length, fluency and excitement of the sketch show how fully articulated this world was, how little he had to stop and think as he wrote it out. 'Well! that was help in need!!', he wrote at the end, before bracing himself to face again 'reality, whole and naked'.[20]

The sketch describes much of the finished work exactly as it was eventually to be. It contains many phrases that were to find their way into the finished text, and several scenes that are worked out to the last detail, notably (as one would expect) the first scene in the hall of the Grail, and Parsifal's return on Good Friday morning. Subsidiary parts of the machinery of the plot are now set out for the first time, almost all of them in full working order and most of them derived in substance from Wolfram. Gurnemanz (spelt Gurnemans in the sketch), the old knight who, chorus-like, gives the audience an enlightening commentary on the drama, who escorts the young Parsifal to the castle of the Grail, and who receives him on his return in the last act, is an amalgam of several characters in Wolfram. He has in him a little of his namesake in Wolfram's poem, the rustic Parsifal's first mentor in courtly behaviour, and a little of Sigune, the sad maiden Parsifal keeps meeting in the forest. He carries the whole significance of the grey knight who asks Parsifal why he is bearing arms on Good Friday, and of the squire who calls him a goose and sends him packing after his failure at the castle of the Grail. But he takes his patient wisdom above all from old Trevrizent, Parzival's hermit uncle, who in Wolfram describes to the youth the power and qualities of the Grail and tells him the story of Amfortas's wound. It is significant, and a neat demonstration of how Wagner transformed the medieval romance into the modern drama, that in Wolfram Trevrizent explains all this to Parzival while in Wagner Gurnemanz explains it only to some young squires and the audience: Wagner's Parsifal has to learn it for himself through experience and compassion.

Titurel, the ancient guardian of the Grail who is kept alive by its magic properties, Wagner took straight from Wolfram, although in Wolfram he is Anfortas's grandfather and not his father. There is a single glimpse of him in Wolfram's castle of the Grail which no doubt stayed in Wagner's mind to be transformed into Titurel's sepulchral voice commanding Amfortas to perform his office. 'Parzival. . .saw, before they closed the door behind them, on a couch in an outer room, the most beautiful old man he had ever beheld. . .He was greyer even than mist.'[21] Wagner adds considerably to what Wolfram tells us of Titurel, allowing him to die as a consequence of Amfortas's refusal to uncover the Grail, and making Parsifal's return to the hall of the Grail coincide with Titurel's funeral ceremony.

Parsifal's first arrival in the land of the Grail — described in the sketch and appearing unchanged in the finished work — is one of the clearest examples of how Wagner took incidents and images from Wolfram and bound them into his dramatic condensation of the story.

In Wolfram's description of Parzival's childhood there is a striking passage which tells of the boy making himself a bow and arrows to shoot birds. 'But whenever he shot a bird whose song was so loud before, he would weep and tear his hair. . .for grief.'[22] (According to an anecdote of Wolzogen's, Wagner said in old age that he had gone out shooting with some other boys at the age of fifteen, had fired one shot, been horrified at the picnic afterwards when a wounded hare limped by, and never again held a gun in his hands.) Later in Wolfram's poem the hero is accompanied by King Arthur's falcon through a snowy forest. He puts up a great flock of wild geese, one of which is wounded by the falcon. Three drops of blood fall on the snow and Parzival stands gazing at them, lost in a trance of love because the red on the white reminds him of the beauty of his wife Condwiramurs whom he has left behind. This is one of Wolfram's most memorable scenes. In Wagner's 1865 sketch — and in the opera — the two Wolfram passages combine to produce this:

While Amfortas is bathing in the holy lake a wild swan circles over his head; suddenly it drops, wounded by an arrow; cries are heard from the lake: general indignation: who dares to kill a beast in this holy place? The swan flaps nearer and falls bleeding to the ground. Parsifal comes out of the forest, a bow in his hand: Gurnemanz. . .reproaches him for the wickedness of his deed. . .What had the swan, seeking its mate, done to him? Does he not feel grief for the noble bird that now with blood-stained feathers lies mute and dying before him? Etc. Parsifal, who has stood silent and rooted to the spot, bursts into tears.

Immediately afterwards, the memory of his deserted mother is revived in him.

So Wagner's Parsifal (and Wolfram's) enters upon pity, guilt and knowledge by causing the death of an innocent creature; and in the Good Friday scene in the third act he attains his goal — the Grail — through a redemption which, though Christian in reference, touches the whole natural world in full accord with Schopenhauer.

More than a quarter of the 1865 sketch consists of the setting out of background information which Wagner is perhaps ordering for the first time in his own mind. The nature and powers of the Grail, the history of Titurel's order of knights into whose care it has been consigned, the story of Klingsor, his self-mutilation, and his magic castle where he holds imprisoned 'the most beautiful women in the world and of all ages'; all this is described with an elaboration which could not appear in full in the actual text of the opera but which was clearly necessary to strengthen Wagner's own hold on the weird and complex inter-connections of his plot.

Klingsor, for example, is said once to have been a pious hermit living in a hut. Failing to conquer desire through prayer and penance, he castrated himself and was nevertheless refused as a knight of the Grail by Titurel because 'renunciation and chastity flow from the inmost

soul, and must not be forced by mutilation.' His mutilation has, however, given him the power to raise in revenge his castle and garden of
sinister beauty in the wilderness where his hut stood. Similarly, Wagner
gives here for the first time a detailed account of the Grail which,
although understood in its Christian sense as a specific relic of Christ,
at the same time retains the magical qualities of Wolfram's mysterious
stone. It keeps its knights alive rather as Freia's apples keep the gods of
Valhalla alive, by supplying them with food and drink, and also (somewhat inconsistently) by the mere sight of itself — hence the ancient
Titurel's prolonged survival. It also issues instructions through the
appearance of writing on its crystal surface. The wretched Amfortas,
compelled by his duty to the knights to expose it in order 'to work the
sacred magic', suffers renewed agony on each occasion, and also of
course maintains life in himself so that he, like Kundry, is condemned
by his own fault to an immortality full of despair. A sign of deliverance
has, however, at last appeared in the form of the words: 'mitleidend
leidvoll wissend ein Tor wird dich erlösen' ('made wise, suffering in
fellow-suffering, a fool will redeem you'), a prefiguring of the arrival of
Parsifal and the action of the opera.

One important aspect of the plot is not yet clear in the sketch. In
the hall of the Grail, as in Wolfram's account, a spear with its tip blood-
stained is carried behind Amfortas, the implication being that it is the
spear which inflicted his wound. Parsifal, however, when threatened by
Klingsor after resisting the wiles of Kundry, 'recognizes the spear with
which Amfortas was wounded', seizes it, and by brandishing it (though
not yet in the sign of the cross) causes Klingsor's castle to collapse in
ruins. On his Good Friday return he drives a spear into the ground and
prays before it, his eyes fixed on the blood-stained tip. Obviously the
second spear, which should logically be the same as the third, cannot be
the same as the first if that is still in the castle of the Grail after the
wounding of Amfortas. Yet the first and third share the blood-stained
tip. In Wolfram there are three significant spears: the one (blood-
stained) in the Grail procession; the one with which the heathen knight
wounds Amfortas; and a quite different spear which Trevrizent gives to
Parsifal for his battles. In the sketch Wagner had not yet thought of
making them all one: it was to be the final piece in the jigsaw of his
plot.

On 2 September 1865, three days after finishing the sketch, he
debated the question in the note-book (known as the Brown Book)
written for Cosima, in which he had also written the sketch before
making a fair copy of it for Ludwig. He is bothered by the confusions

over the spear in Wolfram. Then, progressing from the Christian conception of the Grail, which is not Wolfram's, he goes on: 'The spear belongs, as a relic, with the Grail: in the Grail the blood is preserved which flowed from the Saviour's side, pierced by the spearpoint.' Having given the spear this weighty significance, he outlines two possible schemes for its use in the plot. In the first, Amfortas sets out with the spear to break Klingsor's magic in battle, is seduced, deprived of the spear and wounded with it as he flees. In the second, Klingsor possesses the spear which Amfortas attempts to rescue for the Grail; he is seduced and wounded by Klingsor. In both schemes, 'the healing and salvation of Amfortas is now logical and possible, if the spear can be freed from unholy hands and united with the Grail'. 'Which is better, Cos?', the note ends.[23]

Wagner seems to have forgotten this discussion when, eleven and a half years later, he was working out the final sketch for the work. In Cosima's diary for 30 January 1877 she says: 'At lunch R. told me that he had got over the worst in *Parsifal*; what is important is not the question [Wolfram's healing question that Parzival should have asked at his first encounter with the Grail] but the recovery of the spear.'[24] In fact the first Brown Book plan for the spear went into the final sketch, and into the opera, without alteration; and it had been two decades since Wagner's *Parsifal* had depended on Wolfram's question for its motivation.

The years between 1865 and 1877 saw the completion and overwhelming success of *Die Meistersinger*, the completion of *Siegfried*, the composition of *Götterdämmerung*, the flight of Wagner and later Cosima from Munich to Tribschen and their marriage, the move to Bayreuth, the building of the Festspielhaus and the first performances of the complete *Ring*. All this time *Parsifal* lay in wait for its composer, and now and then he returned to the subject, reading passages of Wolfram to Cosima, or further exploring the ramifications of the legend.

It is difficult to tell from the available evidence how many of the medieval Grail stories he read himself and how much he picked up from studies produced by German Romantic scholars. He probably did read Chrétien de Troyes's *Perceval*, Wolfram's own principal source, in a modern French version: Du Moulin Eckart in his life of Cosima says that Wagner was reading Chrétien in the autumn of 1872, but there is no direct evidence of this in Cosima's diary. He certainly read Johann von Görres's preface to *Lohengrin* that October, from which he learnt of the Celtic origin of the Grail stories and came to the conclusion that Grimm had made too little of the Celtic sources of German mythology. From Görres he adopted the (erroneous) idea that Parsifal's name derived from the Persian for 'pure fool'. By 1875, if not before, he had acquired San-Marte's learned three-volume work *Parcival: Studien,* but he found it 'very abstruse and no use at all' when in 1876 he looked through it in a search for names, presumably for minor characters, the knights and squires in the end left nameless in the opera. San-Marte in 1875 led him to the idea that the Grail 'evolved entirely outside the church, as a peaceful disengagement from it';[25] but as long before as 1848 he himself, in his essay 'Die Wibelungen: Weltgeschichte aus der Sage', had seen the Grail as a spiritual transmutation of the Nibelung's Hoard, the idealized goal of German mythical consciousness quite outside the context of Christianity.

Whatever reading or thinking Wagner did on Parsifal during these years can in any case have made little difference to his plan for the opera which, as we have seen, was in all essentials and most details complete by 1865. Nevertheless, he must from time to time have been both surprised and pleased to find his own intuitive grasp of the Parsifal story confirmed by the findings of scholars and by references to medieval texts unknown to him. The advances in Arthurian scholarship since his death have further ratified this intuitive grasp, which amounts to a remarkable instinct for the springs of myth in the human mind. There is not a single Grail text discussed in, for example, the authoritative collaboration *Arthurian Literature in the Middle Ages* (edited by R. S. Loomis, 1959) that does not somewhere strengthen or support the edifice Wagner constructed from Wolfram, Chrétien and a few nineteenth-century essays, though it is of course impossible now to say exactly where creative intuition took over from magpie assimilation of bits and pieces.

Wagner's decision to give his Grail the full weight of Christian significance is easy to trace: although neither Wolfram nor Chrétien regard the Grail as the cup of the Last Supper, the slightly later continuations of Chrétien by other hands (not differentiated in the text Wagner would have read) have Christianized the imagery of the tale. The first continuation identifies the bleeding spear in the Grail procession with the spear that pierced the side of Christ, while in the second it is said outright that the magic vessel contains the blood of Christ.

More strikingly, the earliest text which tells the full story of Joseph of Arimathea's travels with the cup in which he caught Christ's blood at the deposition was almost certainly not read by Wagner and yet contains details of startling relevance to the opera. This is Robert de Boron's early thirteenth-century *Joseph d'Arimathie.* Here the Grail not only miraculously keeps Joseph alive but has other powers not mentioned in Wolfram or Chrétien. Joseph leaves Judea with a band of fellow-guardians of the Grail, some of whom are guilty of lechery; this causes all of them to suffer from starvation. What is more, Joseph sets up the commemoration of the Last Supper with the Grail in order to detect the guilty, because the ceremony makes the guilty suffer pain.

In later versions of the Grail story, the Christian significance of the vessel and the necessity for chastity in its attendants became commonplace. The French *Queste del Saint Graal,* the source of Malory's Sangrail episodes and hence of Tennyson and the notion of the Grail current among Wagner's contemporaries in Victorian England, has as its hero Galahad rather than Perceval. It shows the adoption of the primitive legend by orthodox Christianity smoothly effected: the Grail ceremony has become a solemn celebration of the eucharist in an austere monastic atmosphere which certainly found its way into Wagner's temple of the Grail, while Perceval's adventures are reduced from Wolfram's shaded ambiguities to a morality-play black and white, and bedecked with Cistercian sermons. It is unlikely that Wagner read the *Queste,* but one episode perhaps reached him in one way or another: the attempted seduction of Perceval by a beautiful temptress who makes him drunk and almost succeeds in overcoming his resistance. He is saved at the last moment by the sight of the cross inlaid in his sword-hilt, and wounds himself in contrition.

More obscure and in many ways more interesting than the Christian interpretation which overlaid the Grail story in its later forms are its pagan Celtic origins. Wolfram probably had a source other than Chrétien. Certain passages in his poem misled scholars, including for a time San-Marte, into the view that Guiot de Provins, another thirteenth-century French poet, was this source, and Wagner and Cosima duly read Guiot (typically adopting in 1875 his line 'En ce siècle puant et horrible' as their 'motto for today').[26] Wolfram's reference to Guiot finding the first source of the Grail story in an Arab manuscript discarded in Toledo may be responsible for Wagner's placing of his Monsalvat in Gothic Spain: Wolfram's Munsalvaesche is more or less located in France, though an interesting twentieth-century theory has it that the geography and many of the proper names in Wolfram derive from Persian legend, and that his identification of the Grail with a precious stone confirms its Persian origin as the pearl of purity. (If this theory is correct, Amfortas's castle was once a Zoroastrian stronghold in Afghanistan and

Klingsor's, ironically, a Buddhist monastery.)[27] However, it is now generally agreed that Celtic Grail legends in Irish, Welsh and Breton, mediated through a lost French text, lay behind the detail in which Wolfram differs from Chrétien. These legends were probably known to Wagner only through the Comte de Villemarque's *Contes des anciens Bretons*, but they contain the deepest roots of his *Parsifal* – roots which he must in some instances have only divined below the surface of Wolfram.

In the most ancient Grail legends several characters and incidents recur in varying forms. Behind the figure of the Maimed King, often the Fisher King, who rules over a Waste Land which can only be restored to fertility by his cure, there is the pagan belief in the connection between the reproductive forces of nature and the potency of the king. The distant ancestors of Amfortas, wounded and hence to blame for the forlorn domain of Wagner's third act, are not only the Welsh Bran (Bron in *Joseph d'Arimathie*, where a fish caught by him lies on the Grail table), Alan King of Brittany, and the Irish Lug (a phantom host in a magic castle), but also Eshmun, Attis and the Ensorcelled Prince in the Arabian Nights who has a lake of magic fish and is paralysed in his lower limbs. In Chrétien this figure is called the Fisher King but has no name; Chrétien implies and Wolfram actually says that he is wounded in the genitals (Wagner's Amfortas, like Christ, is wounded in the side, although Wagner says in the 1865 sketch that Klingsor intended to castrate him). Wagner was aware of the long past of the Fisher King and thought, wrongly, that the name *Le Roi Pescheoir* or *Pêcheur* derived from a confusion with *Le Roi Pécheur*, sinner king.

In the Celtic stories the food-producing vessel with which the king entertains his human guest is a dish or platter, often accompanied by a horn of plenty. It is now thought that a simple verbal misunderstanding – the Welsh *corn* (horn) becoming the French *cors* (body) – was responsible for the Christianization of this pair of objects, a corpse or a severed head accompanying the magic dish or cup in some versions of the story, and eventually a sacred host (corpus Christi). In Wolfram, the magical powers of the Grail stone are renewed every Good Friday when a wafer is placed upon it by a dove from heaven. Wagner, while maintaining the eucharistic orthodoxy of the *Queste*, keeps not only Wolfram's dove and the food-producing properties of the horn of plenty, but also, by coincidence or instinct, the accompanying corpse (Titurel's, in Act III), and even the suggestion of a severed head in Klingsor's reference to Kundry as Herodias. Meanwhile it is Kundry herself whose mysterious origins reach furthest back into the mythical fogs.

In Paris in August 1860, while Kundry was forming in his mind, Wagner was reading Villemarque's *Contes*. Here he will have found a version of *Peredur*, the Welsh *Mabinogion* story of Parsifal, which contains not only a severed head and a bleeding spear (though no Grail) in the castle of a lame king, but also a loathly damsel who later changes into a yellow-haired boy. In the early Irish sagas, which Wagner cannot have known, a crowned maiden serves a human guest with the platter and horn of plenty. She is a personification of Ireland and bears alternate aspects, radiant beauty in Summer, hideous deformity in winter. From her were derived two separate characters in the later romances, the beautiful Grail-bearer and the hideous Grail-messenger (in Wolfram, Repanse de Schoye, Anfortas's sister, and Cundrie). A pagan sense of the symbolic force of the seasons certainly lurks in Wagner's *Parsifal:* the summer lake of the Fisher King; the winter desolation of the Waste Land changing on Good Friday to benign spring; the unnatural florescence of Klingsor's garden evoked by magic from the desert and withering at the touch of virtue. But Wagner was no less in sympathy with the ancient springs of the Grail myth when he deduced, perhaps from the single clue in *Peredur*, the double nature of his Kundry, the Hateful Fée, the repulsive Sovranty of Erin whom the power of love transforms to a beautiful princess. Wolfram, Schopenhauer, and perhaps some deep ambivalence of his own towards women, are responsible for Wagner's hateful fée being good when she is ugly and evil when she is beautiful. Nothing but his own dramatic genius is responsible for her individuality, her fatal *Schadenfreude*, and her pathos as a soul seeking deliverance. He knew that this individuality was what mattered most of all.

In the summer of 1879, when *Parsifal* was composed but not yet scored, Wagner wrote an essay 'Über das Opern-Dichten und Komponieren im Besonderen' ('On the poetry and composition of opera in Particular'). In it he says:

I would recommend a dramatic composer never to think of adopting a text before he is certain it contains a plot, and characters to carry out this plot, that inspire the musician with a lively interest on some account or another. Then let him immediately take a good look at the one character which most strongly appeals to him. . .Let him set it in a dimly lighted place, where he can just see the gleaming of its eyes; if that speaks to him, the shape itself will now most likely begin to move. This may even terrify him, but he must put up with that; at last its lips will part, and a ghostly voice murmurs something quite distinct and able to be grasped, but so unheard of (such as the Stone Guest, and surely the page Cherubino, speaking to Mozart) that he wakes from his dream. . .He has had an idea, a so-called musical motif.[28]

Early in 1877, with the *Ring* festival behind him, Wagner had at last written the final prose sketch, and immediately afterwards the text, of *Parsifal*. It was surely his encounter with the character of Kundry that he remembered in the essay. While writing the final sketch he had seen those gleaming eyes, heard that ghostly voice: 'I have made a note: Kundry can only laugh and scream; she does not know true laughter', he said to Cosima on 16 February 1877.[29] On 27 September, with the prelude just composed, he said: 'I also have some accents for Mademoiselle Kundry; I already have her laughter, for instance.'[30] And in March 1878, while working on the second act, he was worried by the similarity of the scene between Parsifal and Kundry to other scenes he had written, especially the Venusberg scene: 'Mozart had only one single scene like the arrival of the Commendatore'[31] – again, the Stone Guest. Wagner was here afraid of losing in a generalized seduction Kundry's individuality, that dramatic distinctiveness which he had no doubt once glimpsed in the manner described in the essay.

Apart from the clarification of the role played by the spear in the plot, the final sketch and text of *Parsifal* depart scarcely at all from the scheme set out in such detail in 1865. The reasons for the lapse of so many years between the conception of the work and its ultimate completion – the full score was finished in January 1882, thirty-seven years after the Marienbad holiday – are many and various. Other projects intervened and had to be given priority: the urgent inspiration of *Tristan*, the completion of *Meistersinger* for Munich and the king, the tremendous undertaking of the *Ring* which demanded the interrupted labours of nearly thirty years, and the building, financing and operation of the theatre at Bayreuth. But the patient wait for *Parsifal* was also perhaps imposed by the nature and subject of the work.

At the centre of the Grail myth in all its forms is the long journey towards something once seen and not understood, which can at last be recovered only through fidelity and the growth of understanding. Parsifal is, in Wolfram's phrase, 'a brave man slowly wise'. The Grail's attainment is in every sense the end of the story: in the *Queste* and in Malory Galahad dies when he has seen the Grail, and both vessel and spear are taken up to heaven. 'Sithen was there never man so hardy to say that he had seen the Sangrail.' Wolfram's last word on the Grail is subtler but no less resonant. When Parzival's destiny as lord of the Grail has been declared, he tells the whole of Arthur's court that no one can ever fight his way to the Grail 'unless he has been summoned to it by God. This word travelled across all lands, that no fighting could win it, and thus many people desisted from searching for the Grail. For that reason it remains hidden still.'[32]

Wagner's *Parsifal* is a conclusion, the end of a life's work. It is the achievement of an old man who as a young man had seen a creative possibility on the far horizon and through many vicissitudes never lost sight of it. It is also a dramatic unity shaped by a strong and skilful imagination from a diversity of sources, seized here, altered there, discarded somewhere else, over half a lifetime. It is, no less than these, a highly original work for the late nineteenth-century operatic stage, finally put together by an ageing composer suffering from angina and other disorders and needing every protection from the intrusions of the real world. Wagner in 1877 asking Judith Gautier in Paris to send the rich fabrics and exotic perfumes with which he soothed his raw sensibilities as he began to compose the music of *Parsifal* bears an almost uncanny resemblance to Wolfram's Anfortas:

They set about easing his heart's agony. Whenever the sharp and bitter anguish brought the fierce distress upon him, they sweetened the air with perfume. . .musk, theriaca and sandalwood. . .For protection against the poison powdered herbs were strewn over the covers. Quilted, not merely sewn, was the stuff he leaned against, and his mattress was of silk from the east. . .Of joys he had small share.[33]

Wagner was Amfortas in his pain, just as he was Parsifal in his constancy, Kundry in his restless thirst for redemption, and the sorcerer Klingsor. What, exactly, he made of his extraordinary characters, assembled over so long a time and forming in their interaction so strange a drama, a detailed examination of the text of the work will show.

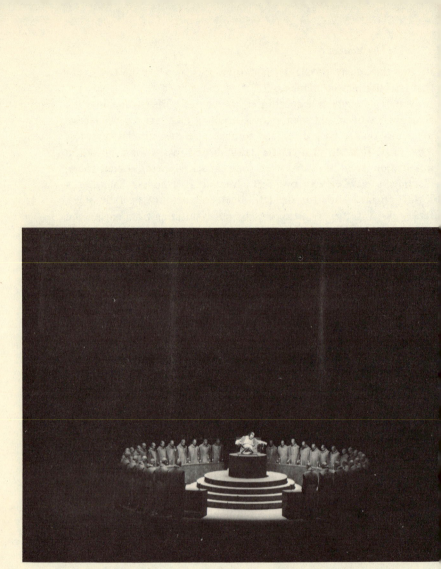

2 Wieland Wagner's set for the Temple of the Grail, Act I Scene 2
and Act III Scene 2; Bayreuth 1951—73, with several modifications to the altar and plinth.

2   Text and synopsis

Das waren hochbedürft'ge Meister,
von Lebensmüh bedrängte Geister:
in ihrer Nöten Wildnis
sie schufen sich ein Bildnis. . .

It was deeply troubled Masters,
their spirits oppressed by the pains of life:
in the desert of their need
they created themselves a form. . .
        R. Wagner, *Die Meistersinger von Nürnberg* Act III Scene 1

'Meine Vorspiele müssen alle elementarisch sein, nicht dramatisch, wie die *Leonoren*-Ouverture, denn dann ist das Drama überflüssig',[1] Wagner said to Cosima in October 1878, when he was composing the prelude to the third act of *Parsifal*. ('My preludes must consist of the elements, and not be dramatic like the Leonora overtures, or the drama becomes superfluous.') So the orchestral prelude to the first act of *Parsifal* does not prefigure the action of the work. It sets out the elements, not of a story or plot but of a situation, a presented contrast between what is calm, clear and ordered, a peaceful goal, on the one hand, and what, on the other, is disturbed and dark, a troubled process. It begins with a long syncopated phrase played in unison on reed instruments and strings. This theme, without either harmony or predictable rhythm, creates at once an atmosphere of strangeness and unease which is not dispelled by the A-flat chords which follow before the theme is repeated an octave higher. By the time the whole passage has been heard again in C minor, and has twice died away into silence, a sense of grieving aspiration has been established, one element in the juxtaposition the prelude sets out. In a programme note Wagner wrote for Ludwig for a performance of the prelude in 1880,[2] he called this theme 'Love', and quoted the words of consecration at the Last Supper. If the passage indeed suggests love, it is love of a particular kind, without joy: 'Liebe als Qual' ('Love as pain'), as Wagner had put it in his 1855 notebook,

25

referring to Parsifal's proposed appearance in *Tristan*.

After this disquieting introduction, the measured, rising phrases of the Dresden Amen, familiar (to a German audience), diatonic and consoling, are simply placed next, bounded by silences, in Wagner's note 'the promise of redemption'. They are succeeded by the tramping rhythms and firm brass chords of the passage Wagner described as 'Faith declaring itself, exalted, unshakeable even in suffering'. The sense of strength and conviction expands, enclosing within it a repeat on the strings only of the Dresden Amen, and reaching a broad climax, a temporary triumph. This passage in its turn dies away, not to silence but to a mutter of timpani and cellos. The opening theme returns, insistent and darkening as it is repeated and raised, and prevails with its unresolved harmonies until the end of the prelude. On a high chord woodwind and violins fade into silence as the curtain rises.

Shadow and light, pain and healing, are not combined or made to interact in the music of the prelude. They are merely set side by side as the given conditions of the drama that is to follow. We do not know, yet, that the winding theme of the beginning and end of the prelude is to be associated with love and suffering, with Amfortas and the loss of the spear, and also with the Last Supper and the Crucifixion. Nor do we know that the Dresden Amen is to narrow its saving significance to the single symbol of the Grail. As the action unfolds we shall learn from what takes place on the stage and from the words the characters sing the particular application of these themes. We shall see and hear the objective correlatives by means of which Wagner, confining to the concrete, as Wolfram had, the subjective abstractions 'Treue' and 'Zweifel' (see p. 3), tells a specific tale in three acts of 'drastic substance', Meanwhile the elements of the prelude, presented in pure contrast though full of the possibilities of conflict and resolution, strike us as the given conditions not only of the drama about to begin but perhaps of life itself. The process of transforming these elements into dynamic actuality starts at once.

The scene is a forest clearing 'shaded and solemn but not gloomy', sloping down to a lake in the background. Gurnemanz, a vigorous old man, and two young squires are asleep under a tree. At the sound of a morning summons (the first phrase of the prelude, played on trombones), Gurnemanz wakes the squires.

> Hört ihr den Ruf? Nun danket Gott,
> dass ihr berufen, ihn zu hören!

> You hear the call? Now thank God

That you are called to hear it!

His words suggest that they are under a particular kind of providential obedience; as the three of them kneel in silent prayer the themes of promise and conviction from the prelude indicate that this is the realm of order and light. We discover immediately, however, that all is not well. Two knights enter, in advance of Amfortas's litter which is being carried to the lake, and a short exchange between one of them and Gurnemanz reveals that the king is sick past ordinary relief. The herb brought for him by the knight Gawan is useless; he can be healed only by a single cure, a single man. These words are given great prominence by the music, foreshadowing the motive that will accompany the words 'der reine Tor', but Gurnemanz breaks off when he is asked to name the healer. So, in twenty-five short, unrhymed lines of text, delivered except for the last two without striking emphasis, we have already learnt of Amfortas's suffering, which oppresses those whom he rules, and of a mysterious stranger who alone can cure him.

To a disturbed passage in the orchestra Kundry appears, wild-eyed and dishevelled, her disarray prefigured in the excitement of knights and squires as they watch her arrival. She has brought balsam from Arabia to ease Amfortas's pain. Saying so, she sinks exhaused to the ground as Amfortas is carried in on his litter. Gurnemanz grieves that the lord of a conquering race should be a slave to sickness: the words 'Herrn' and 'Knecht' are stressed and contrasted in the first rhymed verse in the work, and the music at the same time moves from faith to pain so as to underline Amfortas's fall. The themes of the prelude are already becoming closely identified with specific realities in the drama, and it is in Amfortas that they meet.

Amfortas greets the freshness of the morning in a lyrical passage which is interrupted when he calls for Gawan and is told that the knight has left again on a new search for a cure. His reaction is significant, and contains the first mention of the Grail:

> Ohn' Urlaub! Möge das er sühnen,
> dass schlecht er Gralsgebote hält!

> Without leave! He will have to atone
> for this disobedience to the Grail's command!

The Dresden Amen, hasty and broken off, sounds to these words: Amfortas's illness has destroyed the order he is responsible for maintaining. At once we are given a first hint of the external danger. Amfortas continues, still referring to Gawan:

> Oh wehe ihm, dem trotzig Kühnen,
> wenn er in Klingsors Schlingen fällt!

> Ah, woe to him, bold and stubborn as he is,
> if he should fall into Klingsor's snares!

(Gawan is not mentioned again in the work, but his dashing courage and his association with healing make it likely that he is indeed the secondary hero of Wolfram's poem, who there cures with magic herbs a wounded knight.)

Amfortas's speech, strongly rhymed, ends with the second reference to the promised healer, a little fuller than the first though not yet complete.

> Ich harre des, der mir beschieden:
> 'Durch Mitleid wissend'. . .

> I wait for him who has been assigned to me,
> 'Made wise through compassion'. . .

Amfortas hesitates and continues after encouragement from Gurnemanz: 'der reine Tor' ('The innocent fool'). (Wagner has admirably compressed the phrase from the 1865 sketch: 'mitleiden leidvoll wissender Tor'.) Then, echoing the earlier question as to the name of the healer and referring for the first time to the release he longs for, Amfortas adds:

> Mich dünkt, ihn zu erkennen:
> dürft ich den Tod ihn nennen!

> It seems to me that I know him:
> if I could but name him Death!

Gurnemanz gives Amfortas Kundry's balsam, for which Amfortas thanks her with a noble graciousness, though the music in a moment of dark irony belies his last word as he sings: 'es sei aus Dank für deine Treue' ('Let this be thanks for your constancy'). She restlessly ('unruhig' in Wagner's stage direction) brushes his thanks aside, and he is carried out of sight to the lake in the far background.

Two squires remain with Gurnemanz and the prone figure of Kundry, whom one of the squires taunts for lying there like a wild beast. Her reply tells us something new about the realm of the Grail, whose theme (the Dresden Amen) accompanies her words: 'Sind die Tiere hier nicht heilig?' ('Are not the beasts holy here?').

The succeeding passage, in which Gurnemanz defends Kundry from the suspicion of the squires, is full of irony which can be appreciated only from knowledge that is given later in the work. Without this knowledge, the spectator will gather a sense of mystery and some vague menace surrounding Kundry. But the irony lies in the fact that the squires, who know nothing of her except for her savage appearance, are right to suspect her of evil, while Gurnemanz, who knows of her faithful service to the Grail and guesses at the search for atonement which drives her to do good, is wrong to regard her as harmless. When one of the squires asks:

> So ist's wohl auch jen' ihre Schuld,
> die uns so manche Not gebracht?

> Then was it this very guilt of hers
> which brought upon us so much misery?

he is stating the exact truth, and his words cease in a brief silence which throws them into relief. Even Gurnemanz concedes that disaster has befallen them when Kundry has been mysteriously absent, reappearing unconscious and apparently lifeless in the undergrowth, and he asks her where she was:

> als unser Herr den Speer verlor?
> Warum halfst du uns damals nicht?

> When our master lost the spear?
> Why did you not help us then?

This is the first reference to the spear in the work. It makes its appearance associated with disaster and with Kundry: the orchestra meanwhile weaves beneath the words a sinister chromatic line. 'Ich – helfe nie' ('I never help'), she replies and, again, the squire who insists 'Sie sagt's da selbst' ('She says so herself') is in fact right although Gurnemanz does not know it.

Gurnemanz now tells the squires the story of Amfortas's fall: how he saw Klingsor vanish with the stolen spear as Amfortas lay in the arms of a woman of terrible beauty, 'ein furchtbar schönes Weib', whom Gurnemanz, of course, does not connect with Kundry. Amfortas was wounded: 'Die Wunde ist's, die nie sich schliessen will' ('This wound it is which will never be healed'). So we learn that Amfortas's sickness is caused by a wound inflicted by his own holy spear shamefully lost to Klingsor, the sorcerer. Gurnemanz's account has been accompanied by the chromatic line more and more closely associated with the power of evil, and therefore with Klingsor, and by fragments of the first theme of the prelude, suggesting now the conflation of love, pain and guilt in Amfortas's fall. Two squires return from the lake and Gurnemanz concludes the passage by softly repeating to himself, to different and gentler notes: 'Die Wunde ist's, die nie sich schliessen will!' (This repetition of a verbal phrase to altered music is very unusual in Wagner.)

The four squires sit at Gurnemanz's feet as, in a long narration, he explains the history of Titurel, Klingsor and Amfortas. The information he gives is, of course, necessary to the audience's understanding of the drama, but much of its emotional force has already been not only hinted at in what has taken place on the stage but also brought home in the music. We know what we are to feel about the Grail and its knights and the trouble that has come upon them before we are given their exact history. The special kind of foreknowledge which Wagner's method of exposition has set up gives to the words of Gurnemanz's narration the weight of satisfying confirmation. The passage falls into three parts. The first is the solemn tale of Titurel's commission to protect and serve the Grail, and the spear with which Christ was wounded. Here, at the mention of the Grail as the cup of the Last Supper, the long phrase which began the prelude is heard complete for the first time since the prelude (as if, perhaps, the love and suffering of Christ are reflected only brokenly in the world of the Grail and its wounded king). This section of the narration rises to a climax with the prescription that only an innocent man (der Reine) may become one of the brotherhood of the Grail.

The second part, rapid and nervous in atmosphere, tells how Klingsor, failing to atone for some sin unknown to Gurnemanz, castrated himself in an attempt to attain the Grail. Titurel rejected this unnatural achievement of chastity but Klingsor's evil magic, won from his deed, has enabled him to transform the desert into a garden peopled by beautiful women who lure the Grail knights from their allegiance. The last part of the narration, describing Titurel's conferring of the guardianship of the Grail upon his son Amfortas, and Amfortas's defeat at Klingsor's hands, ties together the first two sections in a swift conclusion. The Grail itself is now threatened by the sorcerer, who already holds the spear seized from Amfortas.

The squires break in for a moment but Gurnemanz has not finished. In a fourth piece of narrative, quiet and accompanied by the measured chords of the Grail theme, he tells how Amfortas has been promised redemption in words emanating from the Grail itself. At last, at its third appearance in the work, we hear the whole prophecy:

> Durch Mitleid wissend
> der reine Tor;
> harre sein,

den ich erkor.

Made wise through compassion
the innocent fool;
wait for him,
the one I summon.

The last three words indicate again the Grail's providential power: as Gurnemanz has said in his narration, those who are called to its service reach it 'auf Pfaden, die kein Sünder findet' ('by paths no sinner can find'). Hence the appalling irony of Amfortas's situation.

The squires begin to repeat the prophecy (in four-part harmony) but before they reach the words 'harre sein', there is, most appropriately placed, a startling interruption. Cries are heard from the lake, and knights and squires rush in, shouting. A wild swan, wounded, flies unsteadily from the lake and drops to the ground. With more irony perceptible only from later knowledge a knight says: 'Der König grüsste ihn als gutes Zeichen' ('The king greeted it as a good omen'). But knights and squires, full of indignation, now lead in Parsifal, a bow in his hand, and when Gurnemanz asks him if it was he who killed the swan, he answers: 'Gewiss! Im Fluge treff ich, was fliegt!' ('Of course! I hit in flight whatever flies!'). Here, in one incident, and one line of text, is Wolfram's careless boy, blundering into an alien realm he has no means of understanding. Yet we have just been told that no one comes to the kingdom of the Grail unless he has been called.

Gurnemanz, in a long passage of gathering emotion, explains to Parsifal what he has done: he has killed a beautiful creature who has done him no harm: 'Was tat dir der treue Schwan?' ('What did the faithful swan do to you?'). Gurnemanz forces the boy to see for himself the congealing blood on the white feathers, the dead eye, 'siehst du den Blick?' ('do you see that look?'), as the music moves from lyrical description of the swan flying over the lake to the dawning of guilt in Parsifal. Parsifal breaks his bow and throws away his arrows. 'Ich wusste sie nicht' ('I did not know'), he says, and in the cross-examination which follows it emerges that he knows nothing, neither where he comes from, who his father is, nor even his own name. This exchange, exposing Parsifal's orphaned dislocation from his origins, has a touching bareness. Attention is drawn to his ignorance of his name by a few bars of a new theme played by the cellos in four parts.

Gurnemanz orders the knights and squires not to leave the king un-attended and they move away bearing the swan on a bier of branches. Although Parsifal has not seen Amfortas carried on his litter, it is im-possible for the audience not to connect the two processions and hence the dead swan with the wounded king. Parsifal, now alone with Gurnemanz and the watching Kundry, is further questioned by the old knight. He remembers his mother's name, Herzeleide (with whom the new theme just heard on the cellos is now associated), and that he was brought up in the wild forest, with only his bow to shoot with. When Gurnemanz asks him why he was not more nobly armed, Kundry interrupts with the information that his mother brought him up a fool to save him from a knightly death like his father's. 'Die Törin!' ('the fool'), she adds, meaning Herzeleide, and laughs for the first time her demoniac *Schadenfreude* laugh. Parsifal remembers more: he followed in vain some glittering knights he saw ride by, and wandered through deserts and mountains defending himself with his bow. He is surprised to hear from Kundry that he is feared: 'Wer fürchtet mich? Sag!' ('Who fears me? Say!'). Kundry replies with a vehemence which suggests the turmoil of her feelings towards Parsifal: 'Die Bösen!' ('The wicked!'). Parsifal again reveals his innocence: 'Die mich bedrohten, waren sie bös?' ('Those who threatened me, were they wicked?').

This passage, since the mention of Herzeleide, has been fast and impetuous, full of the excitement of the adventurous boy expressed in the dotted rhythm of his theme. Now, suddenly, the music almost stops as Parsifal softly sings: 'Wer ist gut?' ('Who is good?'). This is an echo of Wolfram's Parzival who says to Herzeleide, when she refers to God as lord of the birds Parzival grieves for: 'Ah, mother, what is God?' The whole complex of feeling in Wolfram's exchange is present in Wagner's scene, for Gurnemanz answers: 'Deine Mutter, der du entlaufen' ('Your mother, whom you abandoned').

In the 1865 sketch Gurnemanz here accuses Parsifal of injuring both his mother and the swan, and the connection is at once made by Kundry who breaks in again to say that Herzeleide is dead. Parsifal springs in rage at Kundry; he is restrained by Gurnemanz who says, exactly as he did of the swan: 'Was tat dir das Weib?' ('What did the woman do to you?'). There is here perhaps the root of a further confusion in Parsifal's mind, between Herzeleide and Kundry, which will become of deep significance later. Now, as he almost faints with emotional shock, Kundry revives him with water from a spring. Gurnemanz, to a suggestion of the Grail theme, praises her with a further reference to good and evil: 'das Böse bannt, wer's mit Gutem vergilt' ('They conquer evil who repay it with good') (which describes what, eventually, Parsifal will do for Kundry). But Kundry replies, with ironic truth: 'Nie tu' ich Gutes' ('I never do good').

In the whole of this long scene since the rise of the curtain much of the text has been dense with a subtlety almost impossible to appreciate in the theatre, certainly at a first hearing. This particularly applies to the presentation of the character of Kundry. In the 1865 sketch nothing is said of Gurnemanz's narration; the space between Kundry's arrival and the shooting of the swan is devoted entirely to a description of Kundry's ambivalent feelings towards the knights of the Grail, Amfortas in particular. Wagner clearly felt that the information given by Gurnemanz was essential to an understanding of the work: the consequence is that (as Gurnemanz must be largely ignorant of her true nature) Kundry is presented in an elliptical manner which leaves a great deal to the interpretative powers of the singer. For instance Gurnemanz, in accordance with the description of Kundry in the 1865 sketch, says of Parsifal that he has never before met anyone so stupid ('dumm') except Kundry. As Kundry is shown to know more than anyone else of the truth, this remark is incomprehensible unless her hysterical numbness can be suggested by the singer. There are in fact more stage directions for Kundry in this act than there are words for her to sing: she must, for example, suffer at the story of Amfortas's fall, and gaze with mysterious persistence at Parsifal.

She is now overcome with weariness, the sinister import of which is indicated by the coiling theme of Klingsor's magic in the orchestra. Full of terror, but unable to resist, she disappears into the wood to sleep.

The atmosphere changes. Gurnemanz seems to have come to a decision about Parsifal. As the music broadens to a solemn ceremonial pace, he tells him that he is about to lead him to the Grail. 'Wer ist der Gral?' ('Who is the Grail?'), the boy asks, but Gurnemanz answers only that if he is called to it, knowledge of it will come to him. Enough has already been explained about the Grail's power to make sense of Gurnemanz's conclusion that Parsifal has indeed been led here.

A long orchestral passage follows as the two walk in front of a gradually changing scene suggesting a rocky upward path. The illusion and the magical aspect of their journey are confirmed by Gurnemanz's cryptic words:

> Du siehst, mein Sohn,
> zum Raum wird hier die Zeit.

> You see, my son,
> time is here changed to space.

The music which accompanies the transformation is a kind of slow march, sunny and triumphant at the start, darker as the travellers approach the hall of the Grail, when the suffering of Amfortas, in themes now familiar, fades to the summons of deep, knocking bells. When they arrive in the hall, a high, pillared interior, with a vaulted dome, Gurnemanz reveals his hope by quoting the prophecy as he says to Parsifal:

> Jetzt achte wohl und lass mich sehn:
> bist du ein Tor und rein,
> welch Wissen dir auch mag beschieden sein.

> Now watch well and let me see,
> if you are a fool and innocent,
> what knowledge may be vouchsafed to you.

At these words the music rises for the first time in the scene to the full sounding of the Grail theme.

Parsifal stands and watches the whole of the rest of the scene: the effect is to make the audience feel that they are watching what takes place through his eyes.

The knights of the Grail enter the hall singing of the feast about to be celebrated and of its power to refresh 'wer guter Tat sich freut' ('him who delights to do good'): everyone present, the implication is, but Amfortas. When they are all assembled a further procession bears in Amfortas on his litter, while a chorus of altos and tenors, invisible half-way up the dome, sing of the body and blood of the Redeemer, still alive in those purged of sin. The theology of this hymn will be inspected later: the point is in any case more clearly made by the orchestra giving out a version of the Grail theme which breaks at its climax into troubled dissonance. Finally treble voices from the summit of the dome sing in consolation of faith, the hovering dove, and the bread and wine of the feast. These voices fade into a silence full of suspense: in all this sacred whiteness the wounded Amfortas at its centre, the covered shrine of the Grail before him, is the fleck.

The funereal voice of the hidden Titurel, unaccompanied except by soft drum-beats, commands Amfortas to perform his office so that he himself may live and not die. The anguished Amfortas, to the full orchestra, begs Titurel to resume his office and live so that he may die: Wagner's retention, from medieval romance, of the Grail's magic power to confer immortality gives this exchange an element of the macabre which Titurel's reply (belied by the rest of the work) does not dispel: 'Du büss im Dienste deine Schuld!' ('In the Grail's service you atone for your sin!'). 'Enthüllet den Gral!' ('Uncover the Grail!'), Titurel orders, and Amfortas's tortured 'Nein!' produces in itself a powerful sense of shock.

Amfortas now embarks upon a long lament in which he describes the horror of being 'einz'ger Sünder unter Allen' ('the only sinner of them all'), who must nevertheless tend the Grail itself. The storm of emotion with which the lament begins yields to a central passage of calm as he tells of the ray of light that falls on the Grail when it is uncovered. The untroubled statement of the Grail motif is followed at once by the whole of the first theme of the prelude while Amfortas sings of his renewed pain as his sinful blood courses in reponse to the revealed mystery of the Grail. It is impossible to label this theme with any single phrase. Commentators usually refer to it as the Love Feast motif, but it really signifies no more and no less than the ambivalent core of the work: the suffering of Amfortas before the means of salvation he has forfeited, and also the suffering of Christ as the neglected means of salvation. Some of this complexity is indicated in the words of Amfortas's lament as he sings of the spear which wounded both himself and Christ, and of the blood which flowed from Christ's wound,

> ob der Menschheit Schmach,
> in Mitleids heiligem Sehnen.

> for man's disgrace
> in compassion's holy longing.

Amfortas's own longing is not free of sinful passion. When he sings of his blood,

> ewig erneut aus des Sehnens Quelle
> das, ach! keine Büssung je mir stillt,

> ever renewed from the source of longing
> that, alas!, no atonement can ever still in me,

he is close to Tannhäuser's confession of 'Sehnen, das kein Büssen noch gekühlt' ('Longing, which no atonement ever cools').

The lament subsides, however, after desperate cries for mercy (at which the otherwise motionless Parsifal presses his hand to his heart), into a quieter and slower appeal for forgiveness and a holy death; and at once the concealed choir in the dome sings the prophecy of the innocent fool for whom Amfortas is to wait. At last, after further prompting from the knights and Titurel, the Grail is uncovered and lit by a ray from above as Amfortas raises it in his hands and blesses with it the bread and wine on the altar. Meanwhile the words of consecration are sung by the high voices in the dome to the first theme of the prelude, played once on the cellos and then twice repeated in rising succession exactly as it was at the opening of the whole work.

As the glow of the Grail fades and daylight returns, squires distribute the bread and wine (in the 1865 sketch these were to have appeared miraculously during the darkness); the knights sit down to eat. Parsifal ignores Gurnemanz's sign to take a place beside him. In a lightening of tension, the choir accompanies the feast with a remote, clear hymn, almost liturgical in character, which seems to rise above the darkness of Amfortas's agony. The knights join in a chorus of martial optimism which shares with the medieval templars (whom Wolfram identified with the Grail knights) something of the incongruity latent in the idea of warriors of Christ. But the central mystical significance of the Grail is restored by a noble crescendo in which the Dresden Amen, to the words 'Selig im Glauben und Liebe' ('Blessed in faith and love'), rises from the depths of bass voices and trombones to the heights of trebles and flutes.

The ceremony complete, the knights embrace, and, carrying Amfortas, who has taken no part in the meal and whose wound is bleeding, leave the hall of the Grail in procession. The music resumes the slow march of the transformation, broken by references to Amfortas's pain and one echo of the prophecy of the innocent fool. When the hall is empty the prophecy motive is heard again on the oboe as Gurnemanz turns to the motionless Parsifal, who has stood transfixed throughout the scene: 'Weisst du, was du sahst?' ('Do you know what you have seen?'). Parsifal again presses his hand to his heart, as he did at Amfortas's cry for mercy, and shakes his head. Gurnemanz angrily concludes: 'Du bist doch eben nur ein Tor!' ('So you are no more than a fool!') and pushes him outside with a rough comment about leaving swans in peace and finding a goose instead.

As the curtain falls a solitary voice from the dome sings the prophecy once more and the choir repeats, to the Grail theme, 'Selig im Glauben'.

After the prevailing slowness of the first act, the second opens with a swift, frenetic prelude, shot through with the rapid descending scale of Kundry's laugh. We are in a different world: faith and suffering love have been left behind with the music of the first act. Here Klingsor, Kundry and Parsifal himself — none of them referred to in the first-act prelude — contend for victory in encounter and convulsive action; it is in this central act, and between these three characters, that the drama will reach its crisis.

The curtain rises upon the inner keep of Klingsor's magic castle where he sits in near-darkness before a metal mirror, surrounded by the paraphernalia of sorcery. The scene suggests at once the narrow self-regarding realm of evil, in contrast to the Grail's kingdom of light in which even the beasts were holy.

'Die Zeit ist da!' ('The time has come!'), Klingsor begins, with something of the same momentous force as that with which the Flying Dutchman landed and announced: 'Die Frist ist um' ('The hour is near'), except that it is Kundry who shares the Dutchman's periodic need to seek salvation from a curse. Klingsor sees in his mirror Parsifal approaching the castle and, to shivering scales in the orchestra, he summons Kundry from sleep, calling her:

> Namenlose,
> Urteufelin! Höllenrose!
> Herodias warst du, und was noch?
>
> Nameless one,
> Devil of old! Rose of Hell!
> You were Herodias, and what else?

After this reference to her long history of doomed reincarnation, she appears in the darkness with a dreadful scream and responds with broken words of grief to Klingsor's taunts about her futile serving of the Grail knights whom she herself has ruined. They are all fallible, he tells her, but today the most dangerous must be confronted, he whom innocence shields.

In the powerfully dramatic exchange which follows, the relationship between the magician and his instrument of evil becomes clear. Klingsor is Kundry's master because only he can resist her power. 'Bist du keusch?' ('Are you chaste?'), she mocks him, laughing, in her turn, and in a black reflective passage Klingsor reveals his own inexhaustible suffering. He castrated himself in order to conquer desire and so become a knight of the Grail, but Titurel drove him out nevertheless. In revenge he has destroyed Titurel's son and soon will guard the Grail itself. The audience knows these facts already, but Wagner here, characteristically, re-presents them as they seem to Klingsor himself and the passage has a pathos akin to that of Milton's Satan. Kundry in reply mourns the weakness of all the Grail knights who keep her locked in her misery by failing to resist her. As Klingsor, with a charged mixture of contempt and admiration, describes the bold arrival of the handsome Parsifal, whose simple heroic motive is heard through the fragmented music which has accompanied the scene, Kundry becomes more and more agonisingly torn between her desire to avoid the seduction before her and her desire to escaped into 'ewiger Schlaf' ('eternal sleep'), which can be achieved only through the failure of just such a seduction. At last, as Klingsor tells of Parsifal's successful fight with the captive knights of the castle, Kundry bursts into hysterical laughter, screams and disappears.

With triumphant delight Klingsor watches Parsifal reach the rampart of the castle and gloats over the prospect of his imminent fall:

> die Reinheit dir entrissen,
> bleibst mir du zugewiesen!
>
> innocence snatched from you,
> you will stay to be my slave!

After this threat the sorcerer and his tower sink quickly out of sight and the scene changes at once to a luxuriant garden full of tropical vegetation. The sinister speed of this magic growth forms another contrast to the first act, where a gradual transformation took place in an atmosphere of sombre mystery.

The scene between Klingsor and Kundry has presented with masterly economy not only the trap set for Parsifal by the Grail's evil enemy but the ambiguous horror of Kundry's situation. When she cries 'Sehnen... Sehnen!' ('Longing!'), or moans in despair at Klingsor's insidious 'Er ist schön, der Knabe' ('the boy is handsome'), her desire is both for Parsifal and for extinction, although she may only attain the second through the thwarting of the first. All this, which Wagner explained to himself in pages of prose in 1865, is concentrated into a very few lines of taut and, except for Klingsor's short moment of melancholy, unrhymed text.

As soon as the magic garden has appeared, however, the tension slackens. Flower Maidens gather, looking for the knight who has scattered their lovers, and toss snatches of song, soft and high, from one to the other. 'Wer ist der Frevler?' ('Who is the culprit'), some of them sing, echoing oddly the knights of the first act in their outrage at the murder of the swan. When Parsifal jumps down into their midst and tells them how pretty they are, their complaints turn to gay flirtation and, in alternating groups, they rush away and return decked with flowers to dance round him to an archly sweet waltz tune. Wagner directs (perhaps somewhat optimistically) that this scene should be played 'wie in anmutigem Kinderspiele' ('with the charm of a children's game'), but his dramatic sense gave the sung words a sickly chromatic lilt which does not allow the audience to forget entirely that these are Klingsor's she-devils. Parsifal is no more than dazed by their antics, rebuking them mildly for quarrelling over him. At last he loses patience and is about to escape when suddenly, striking through the light exchanges of the Flower Maidens, Kundry's voice is heard calling, with electrifying effect: 'Parsifal! Weile!' ('Parsifal! Stay!').

This is the first time in the opera that the name of the prophesied saviour has been heard: Gurnemanz avoided the question and Amfortas would have had him called Death, while the boy himself was ignorant of his own name. Kundry's call, 'Parsifal' sung to the notes associated with the words 'reine Tor', has, of course, the air of fairy-story destiny which Wagner remembered from Wolfram. It also carries a full load of Wagnerian psychological complexity. Parsifal stands amazed:

> Parsifal?
> So nannte träumend mich einst die Mutter.
>
> Parsifal?
> So once in a dream my mother called me.

Before the words 'die Mutter' there is a brief silence. All the tension which the Flower Maidens dispelled, Kundry's call has now restored to the drama. She sends them away, 'früh welkende Blumen' ('soon-fading flowers') – unlike herself – and they leave with half-fearful, half-laughing farewells.

Parsifal is still transfixed, wondering if the garden itself is a dream, while Kundry becomes visible, unrecognizably changed to a woman of great beauty lying on a couch of flowers. The significance of her knowledge of his name is pressed home. She tells him that his father, dying in Arabia, gave him the name of Parsifal, 'Fal parsi, dich reinen Toren', before he was born. (Wagner believed that 'Parsifal' or 'Fal parsi', meant 'pure fool' in Persian.) She adds, playing on her own name and emphasizing the knowledge he is about to gain:

> ihn dir zu künden, harrt ich deiner hier:
> was zog dich her, wenn nicht der Kunde Wunsch?
>
> to tell you this I waited here for you:
> what drew you here, if not the wish for knowledge?

Then, to the winding chromatic line of Klingsor's evil power, which soon turns to the theme associated with Parsifal's mother Herzeleide, Kundry tells him, in the most sensual manner, the story of his own childhood, of his mother's love for her fatherless child, and of her guarding him from the world of strife. With irony the word *Kunde* is used again:

> Nur Sorgen war sie, ach! und Bangen:
> nie sollte Kunde zu dir her gelangen.

> She was only anxious and afraid
> lest you should ever find your way to knowledge.

The music becomes more and more passionate as Kundry describes the child returning to his mother's embrace. After a climax reached as Kundry asks him if he perhaps feared Herzeleide's kisses, the orchestral accompaniment dies away to bare clarinets in major seconds and she tells him of the day when he did not return to his mother, after which she sickened and died of grief.

Parsifal collapses in despair at Kundry's feet, calling himself for the first time a fool, and at once she tells him of the consolation for sorrow that there is in love. He appears not to hear; as he wonders what else, having forgotten his mother, he might also have forgotten, the music of Amfortas's suffering sounds momentarily in the orchestra. Kundry winds her arm round his neck while, with seductive sophistry, she tells him of the value of repentance and understanding and, in almost the same breath, that he must learn of his parents' love for each other by receiving the kiss from her that his mother sends him now. Kundry kisses him on the mouth, to the full sounding of the chromatic theme of Klingsor's power, which is overtaken, before the kiss is over, by the music associated with the suffering of Amfortas. To a rending downward figure in the orchestra Parsifal tears himself from Kundry, crying, 'Amfortas! Die Wunde! Die Wunde!' ('The wound!'), and pressing his hand to his heart as he had, twice, in the temple of the Grail.

This extraordinary moment, carefully prepared in the long exposition of the first act, is the turning-point of the work. Parsifal is overcome with a revelation of knowledge, understanding, compassion and remorse, and his stormy lament is poured out to a swift, tormented accompaniment which refers again and again to the scene in the Grail hall.

> Die Wunde sah ich bluten —
> nun blutet sie in mir!
>
> I saw the wound bleeding —
> now it bleeds in me!

he sings, and then identifies the horrifying sensation: 'Das Sehnen, das furchtbare Sehnen' ('The longing, the dreadful longing'). There is here no doubt as to what 'Sehnen' means, and at the climax of the passage, on a tremendous chord, he cries out: 'O! Qual der Liebe!' ('O agony of love!'). He then remembers the Grail itself and its redemptive peace, and feels with Amfortas the guilt of the stain on its purity. He seems even to hear the voice of Christ himself calling from his profaned sanctuary:

'Erlöse, rette mich
aus schuldbefleckten Händen!'

'Redeem, rescue me
from guilt-defiled hands!'

At this realization Parsifal blames himself for his blindness and ends his lament: 'Wie büss ich, Sünder, solche Schuld?' ('How may I, a sinner, atone for such guilt?').

Kundry's reaction to all this (carefully described in the stage direction) is amazement followed by passionate adoration. She bends over Parsifal again, but as she does so he describes her caresses in a kind of trance, identifying himself with Amfortas to the point where, as she tries to kiss him for the second time, he thrusts her away from him, telling her with great force to leave him for ever. At this she is swept into a passionate confession in which she herself, for the first and only time in the work, relates the full horror of her fate. Just as even Klingsor had his moment of self-revelation, so now Kundry, whom so far we have learnt to understand only through the hints and taunts of others, speaks from within the complexities of her tragic character. If Parsifal can feel only the miseries of others, she begins, then let him feel hers. In a passage of great emotional density she sings:

Bist du Erlöser,
was bannt dich, Böser,
nicht mir auch zum Heil dich zu einen?
Seit Ewigkeiten – harre ich deiner
des Heilands, ach! so spät!
den einst ich kühn geschmäht.

If you are a redeemer,
what forbids you, evil man,
from becoming one with me for my salvation?
Through endless ages I have waited for you
the saviour – ah! so late!
whom once I dared to scorn.

The confusion of her feelings about Parsifal (*Erlöser*, *Böser*), and the confusion of him with Christ persist throughout the rest of the scene. Here she echoes the prophecy Amfortas received, in the words 'harre ich deiner', and goes on, wild with grief, to tell of the curse which afflicts her, her voice trailing over a complete silence as she sings the phrase: 'endlos durch das Dasein quält!' ('It tortures me without end through this existence!'). Then, in a passage in which the identification of Parsifal with Christ is pushed to an even greater intensity, she describes her primal sin, her mocking laugh, and the look which Christ turned upon her. Both look and laugh are repeated every time a sinner falls into her arms; and, in a return to the instinct for seduction which belies all she has just said, she ends with a plea for redemption in one hour of love with him whom she knew (as Christ) to be the saviour.

To these despairing confusions Parsifal replies with the clarity of his new-found understanding. If he yielded to her, they would both be damned for ever. He is indeed to bring about her salvation but only in despite of her desire, not through it. His words are rapid and firm, their conviction faltering only when, overcome by the misery of her plight, he utters a cry of desolation – a desolation which, true to his compassion, is hers rather than his own:

> O Elend, aller Rettung Flucht!
> O, Weltenwahns Umnachten:
> in höchsten Heiles heisser Sucht
> nach der Verdammnis Quell zu schmachten!
>
> O sorrow, flight from all salvation!
> O deep night, folly of the world:
> the burning search for supreme redemption
> that still longs for the source of damnation!

Now turned wholly back from self-knowledge to seduction, Kundry passionately argues that if one kiss revealed so much to him, an hour of her full love would transform him to godhead. Her hysterical torment is underlined by a snatch of the Flower Maidens' coyly flirtatious tune, followed by a muffled reference to the prophecy of the innocent fool as she twists its words to the opposite of their true meaning. Parsifal continues to resist her and at last offers her love and redemption indeed if she will show him the way to Amfortas. He refers to the mystery surrounding the path back to the Grail castle, but there is irony in his request since Kundry has already in a deeper sense shown him, precisely, the way to Amfortas. The mention of Amfortas topples Kundry into a last spasm of rage and mocking laughter as she remembers his fall, to his own spear. But when Parsifal asks who dared to wound him with the holy weapon she twists yet once more. 'Er' ('He'), she begins, and we expect her to mean Klingsor, but to a change of harmony she repeats 'Er' and continues: 'der einst mein Lachen bestraft' ('who once punished my laughter'), and it is clear that for her it is Christ who has damned both herself and, through her, Amfortas. In a last plea for mercy in the embrace that would be fatal, she cries: 'Mitleid! Mitleid mit mir!' ('Have pity! Pity on me!') – appealing to the very quality through which Parsifal must become wise. But she goes on:

Nur eine Stunde mein!
Nur eine Stunde dein!

For a single hour mine!
For a single hour thine!

and her voice rises to a final phrase of clinging chromatic sweetness.
But Parsifal again thrusts her away and in fury she now calls for help.
She also condemns Parsifal with a curse of her own, uttered to music of
ferocious violence, to wander through the world never finding the path
he seeks. The curse is not only given by her, it is her own wilderness
to which she dismisses him:

Irre! Irre!
mir so vertraut —
dich weih ich ihm zum Geleit!

Wander! Wander!
You who were entrusted to me,
I consign you to its thrall!

At her cries for help Klingsor has appeared on the rampart. With a
sneering threat to 'the fool', he hurls the spear at Parsifal, but it remains
poised above the boy's head. Parsifal seizes the spear, and, still possessed
with his impregnable clarity, moves it in the sign of the cross to banish
Klingsor's magic as the Grail theme rings out in triumph. To a single bar
of a descending figure on the violins the castle crashes to the ground
and the garden withers to a desert strewn with faded flowers, in an
emblematic dying of evil before the power of goodness. Klingsor
vanishes. Kundry collapses with a scream; and Parsifal, as he moves
swiftly away, turns to address Kundry in a bleak little phrase which
seems to show that their destinies are still connected:

Du weisst,
wo du mich wiederfinden kannst!

You know
where you can find me again!

To a last stormy swirl and a final bang from the orchestra, the curtain
falls.

In the third act we return to the kingdom of the Grail, but not, in any
sense, immediately. The orchestral prelude, even more strongly *elementarisch* than that to the first act, concerns the passing of time and
the constantly thwarted struggle to regain what has been lost, to mend
what has been shattered. It begins wearily, with a passage for strings

only, in which a protracted, dark theme of halting rhythm and shifting chromatic harmony gives way to the driven, jerky rhythm of the curse Kundry put upon Parsifal at the end of the second act. These chopped rising figures fade indeterminately and are succeeded by others, broken attempts, as it were, at the rising chords of the Grail theme. Woodwind and horns join the strings in the last of these attempts, but it rises, in crescendo, only to a tearing dissonance which disintegrates in the downward chromatic figure of Kundry's laughter. In the rest of the prelude, melancholy and restless music besets the theme of the saving prophecy, the *reine Tor,* which is now damaged in rhythm and complicated in harmony as if Parsifal himself were almost overcome by the difficulties of his wandering journey. The prelude fades to an uneasy chord broken by three drum-beats and short woodwind phrases as the curtain rises. An extraordinary impression of stress and exhaustion, and of the dragging weight of years, has been created, specific because of the significance acquired over two acts by some elements in the music, and yet also abstract, the musical epitome of frustrated effort. The prelude lasts for forty bars which take approximately three and a half minutes to perform.

The scene is a flowery spring landscape at the forest's edge in the early morning. Kundry's voice is heard, in a low moan. Gurnemanz, much older than in the first act and dressed as a hermit, emerges from a small hut and listens. His first words indicate that we are back in the land where even beasts are sacred and where all the suffering is human:

> Von dorther kam das Stöhnen;
> so jammervoll klagt kein Wild,
> und gewiss gar nicht am heiligsten Morgen heut.

> The groaning came from over there.
> No beast cries so wretchedly,
> and least of all on this holiest morning.

The last three words are sung to a heroic phrase which sets the special quality of this particular day behind the awakening that follows.

Kundry's voice moans again from the undergrowth. Gurnemanz crosses the scene, sees her, and pulls her from the bushes. His few words not only suggest that the miseries of her past have at last ended, but also, with their echo of Klingsor's 'Die Zeit ist da', point the contrast between this awakening and that at the beginning of the second act.

> Das winterlich rauhe Gedörn
> hielt sie verdeckt: wie lang schon? —
> Auf! — Kundry! — Auf!

Der Winter floh, und Lenz ist da!

The rough thorns of winter
have kept her hidden: and for how long?
Up, Kundry, up!
Winter has fled, and spring is come!

Kundry is stiff and cold but Gurnemanz gradually revives her. When she opens her eyes, to a fresh ascent of the Grail theme in the orchestra, she shatters its climax (a dissonance, as in the prelude) with a scream that seems to purge her of her wildness. She is dressed as in the first act, as a penitent, but she is paler and quiet, and she at once sets to work like a serving maid. In reply to Gurnemanz's questions she sings only the single repeated word: 'Dienen. . .dienen' ('To serve. . .to serve'), a broken utterance which is her only one in the entire act, although she is on the stage for almost the whole of it.

Gurnemanz, telling her that there is little work now for her to do in the kingdom of the Grail, hints at the disarray into which the knights have fallen. He sees her altered manner, and, attributing the change in her to the holy day, says, with an irony that will be revealed by what is about to happen:

O Tag der Gnade ohne Gleichen!
Gewiss, zu ihrem Heile
durft ich der Armen heut
den Todesschlaf verscheuchen.

O day of mercy without compare!
Truly for her salvation
I was able today to chase
from poor Kundry the sleep of death.

To a gentle passage in the strings which will be expanded later, Kundry fetches water from the spring. But Gurnemanz sees someone approaching and Parsifal's bold theme, now slowed and darker, is heard as he emerges from the forest in black armour with his helmet closed and seats himself on the mound by the spring. The music accompanying his arrival is weary and hesitant, interrupted by Gurnemanz's noble greeting, 'Heil dir, mein Gast!' ('Hail to you, guest'), but emphasizing, with its dotted, halting rhythm, the exact appropriateness of the old man's next words: 'Bist du verirrt, und soll ich dich weisen?' ('Are you lost, and may I guide you?'). Parsifal remains silent. Gurnemanz tells him, to the first completed sounding of the Grail theme in the act, though a mild and far from triumphant one, that he has reached a sacred place. Parsifal knows neither where he is nor that this is Good Friday when no man should be armed; Gurnemanz's sad surprise at this forlorn head-shaking conveys something of Parsifal's distant wanderings:

> Ja! Woher kommst du denn?
> Bei welchen Heiden weiltest du?
>
> Nay, whence do you come, then?
> With what heathens have you lived?

Gurnemanz orders him to lay down his weapons on this day, when the Lord redeemed the sinful world. Very slowly, and to music of sorrowful heaviness, Parsifal plants his spear into the ground, lays shield, sword and helmet beneath it, and then kneels before it in prayer, his theme sounding faintly through a sustained C sharp on the strings. Gurnemanz recognizes him (as does Kundry, nodding agreement) as the boy who once killed the swan, the fool whom he angrily drove away; and as he does so the orchestra returns to the atmosphere of the first act, not with the prophecy but with the first theme of all, the theme associated with the suffering of Amfortas, of the Grail and of Christ himself. With an emphasis pointing to the substance of this whole scene Gurnemanz asks: 'Ha! Welche Pfade fand er?' ('Ah! By what paths did he come?'). Then he recognizes the spear, and, with deep emotion which leaves us uncertain whether he refers to the holiness of Good Friday or of the spear's return, he cries:

> O! Heiligster Tag,
> an dem ich heut erwachen sollt!
>
> O holiest day,
> to which I have this morning woken!

Parsifal rises and, recognizing Gurnemanz, sings quietly, after a pure enunciation of the Grail theme in the orchestra: 'Heil mir, dass ich dich wiederfinde' ('I am glad that I have found you again'). The accent of the vocal line falls, warmly, on the word 'dich'. After all that the music has told us of Parsifal's wanderings, and after his long silence on the stage, these words, echoing his words to Kundry at the end of the second act, are touchingly simple.

It may perhaps be helpful to examine the passage which follows, and which leads up to the first of the act's great climaxes, in rather more detail than is possible for the whole of this synopsis. As an example of how Wagner achieves the manifold complexity of his expressive ends it is almost arbitrarily chosen: many short sections of this scene could teach the same lessons.

Gurnemanz refers briefly to his forlorn state:

So kennst auch du mich noch?
Erkennst mich wieder,
den Gram und Not so tief gebeugt?

Then you also still know me?
You recognize me again
whom grief and need have bowed so low?

The point is reinforced by a sad little phrase, exposed for a mere bar,
on the first violins, before Gurnemanz asks: 'Wie kamst du heut?
Woher?' (How have you now come, and from where?'). A soft diminished seventh chord on the horns draws attention to Parsifal's reply, as
if he were taking a deep breath. This is his first extended utterance in
the act. For five bars he describes his unhappy wandering:

Der Irrnis und der Leiden Pfade kam ich;
soll ich mich denen jetzt entwunden wähnen. . .

By error and by paths of suffering I came;
can I now believe myself delivered from them. . .

(The unusual word 'Irrnis' retains the sense of physical straying; it was
this to which Kundry condemned him with her cry 'Irre!') These lines
are sung to the halting syncopated figure, on the upper strings, associated
with his lostness; no word except, for emphasis and to echo Gurnemanz's
recent question, 'Pfade', comes on the first beat of the bar, and in the
bass, only the cellos sound on the beat, with a quiet tread in contrary
motion to the figure in the violins and violas. Parsifal's question moves
towards hope:

da dieses Waldes Rauschen
wieder ich vernehme,
dich guten Greisen neu begrüsse?

now that I hear again
the rustle of this forest,
and greet you, good old man, once more?

The change of mood is signalled in the orchestra by even softer horn
chords in the major, and by an accompanying phrase on the first violins
which is a sunny equivalent of the phrase that had interrupted
Gurnemanz. But the sunshine lasts for only four bars. To a new,
melancholy string figure, Parsifal hesitates:

Oder – irr' ich wieder?
Verändert dünkt mich alles.

Or – am I still astray?
All seems to me changed.

Parsifal's description of his travels, his relief at his arrival, and the doubt produced by his perception of the decay about him have been conveyed in seven short lines of text and twelve bars of music scored for strings, horns and one bassoon.

Gurnemanz, pressing on at once with his questions (his first word falls on the eighth quaver of the same bar of which Parsifal's last syllable was on the sixth), asks: 'So sag', zu wem den Weg du suchtest?' (But say, to whom were you seeking the way?'). Even this fragment of dramatic machinery has its point: the ignorant Parsifal of Act I had asked Gurnemanz '*Wer* ist der Gral?' ('*Who* is the Grail?'). The echo of this confusion in 'zu *wem*' here, when we know that the Grail is the object of Parsifal's quest, adds, however slightly, to the sense of connection between the healing of Amfortas and that of the Grail.

After half a bar of absolute silence, Parsifal bursts into his recollection of the despairing Amfortas. 'Zu ihm' he sings, in an upward leap of a minor ninth, the 'ihm' falling on the first beat of the next bar and on an anguished chord, still scored for strings, horns and now two bassoons. This is the beginning of Parsifal's longest utterance in the whole scene and the only account he gives of all that has passed, for him, between Klingsor's defeat and his own reappearance in the kingdom of the Grail. Much of the music is that of the third-act prelude, fragmented and rearranged but now given by the words the specific reference it then lacked.

The stormy first eight bars, full of *fortepiano* markings, swift crescendos and the interval characteristic of the prophecy motive, accompany Parsifal's memory:

> Zu ihm, des tiefe Klagen
> ich törig staunend einst vernahm,
> dem nun ich Heil zu bringen
> mich auserlesen wähnen darf.

> To him, whose deep lament
> I heard once in foolish astonishment,
> now to bring him healing
> I dare to think myself chosen.

The chief stress of these eight bars falls on the word 'Heil'. Both here and in what follows it is important to remember that the German 'Heil' contains the sense of 'health', 'wholeness' and 'holiness', and is also the ordinary theological term for 'grace' in the sense closest to 'salvation': 'der Heiland' is the Saviour (Christ). In the central and longest section (nineteen bars) of Parsifal's speech, the words 'Heil' and, to a lesser extent, 'Pfad' are used, in the same way that Wagner uses fragments of music, to seize and direct the audience's attention.

> Doch – ach! –
> den Weg des Heiles nie zu finden,
> in pfadlosen Irren
> trieb ein wilder Fluch mich umher:
> zahllose Nöte,
> Kämpfe und Streite,
> zwangen mich ab vom Pfade,
> wähnt' ich ihn recht schon erkannt.

> But ah!
> never to find the way of salvation,
> in pathless straying
> a savage curse drove me about:
> countless dangers,
> battles and conflicts
> forced me from the path
> even when I thought I had found the right one.

'Den Weg des Heiles' is a phrase full of significant ambiguity: the healing, or redemption, at stake is Parsifal's as much as it is Amfortas's. These words are sung to the strained, frustrated music of the third-act prelude, the five rapid rising notes (two semiquavers and a triplet, slurred) associated with Kundry's curse changing, in the bar of the last line quoted, to four rising but accentuated semiquavers, suggesting the Dresden Amen weakened and injured. The mood of the words now alters with a new sentence, beginning: 'Da musste mich Verzweiflung fassen' ('Then I was forced into the grip of despair'). But the music, pushed along by the pressure of the struggle described, takes a bar to catch up: the last set of rising semiquavers, in a fierce crescendo in which the woodwind and a single horn join the strings, accompanies the held high F sharp to which Parsifal sings the second syllable of 'Verzweiflung'. After this peak of fear, the vocal line rises twice more in pain, to F natural (on the first syllables of 'hüten' and 'wahren'), as Parsifal describes his efforts to retain the holiness of the means of salvation ('Heiltum' – the first syllable of which is stressed by a dotted crotchet on the first beat of a bar) that he has won.

> Da musste mich Verzweiflung fassen,
> das Heiltum heil mir zu bergen,
> um das zu hüten, das zu wahren
> ich Wunden jeder Wehr mir gewann;
> denn nicht ihn selber
> durft' ich führen im Streite;

> Then I was forced into the grip of despair,

that I might fail to keep safe the saving treasure,
to guard and preserve which
I won wounds from every weapon;
for this itself
I dared not wield in conflict;

The awe in which Parsifal holds the 'Heiltum' is emphasized by the silence in the orchestra, almost a whole bar long, to which he sings the words of the last line: only on 'Streite' is he rejoined by the strings. This emphasis marks the end of the central, hurried and anxious, section of his speech, which now moves into its brief, heroic conclusion:

unentweiht
führ' ich ihn mir zur Seite,
den ich nun heim geleite,
der dort dir schimmert heil und hehr:
des Grales heil'gen Speer.

unprofaned
I have carried it at my side,
and now I bear it home,
shining safe and sound before you,
the Grail's holy spear.

There has been no rhyme since the rise of the curtain. Now, picking up from 'Streite', and resolving the 'conflict' which the word means, Parsifal sings two strong, affirmative lines which rhyme with it, and the dotted rhythm of 'heim geleite' is at once taken up by the bass (lower strings and bassoons) so that the triumphant final couplet is accompanied by a solid marching beat in the orchestra. The music moves into a resounding full close: the first syllable of '*heil*'gen', held for three whole beats, is the longest note Parsifal has yet sung. The last touch to the climax is the word 'Speer', uttered by Parsifal for the first time and, coming at the very end of his complicated paragraph, seeming to confirm his victorious safe-keeping of the sacred weapon.

With a swiftness and emotional density that defy translation into words, Wagner crowns the climax with the first two bars of the first theme of the whole work, on two horns and a trombone, its darkness cutting across Parsifal's pride with something like the effect, in *Die Meistersinger,* of Sachs's melancholy after 'Wach'auf!'. But the darkness is routed: the two bars lead to a tremendous chord of exultant resolution on the first beat of a third bar, and Gurnemanz breaks into a joyful exclamation:

O Gnade! Höchstes Heil!
O! Wunder! Heilig, hehrstes Wunder!

O mercy! Most high salvation!
O wonder! Holy, highest wonder!

Six bars of celebration die quickly away; triumph has now been added to the complex of connotations that the first theme has already acquired. There follows at once a gentle, though full enunciation (flutes, oboes, bassoons and brass are joined and then succeeded by four-part clarinets and strings) of a version of the Faith theme that has not been heard since Act I. There it accompanied Gurnemanz's account of the original assignment, by angels, of the Grail to the guardianship of Titurel. The point is enforced by the beautiful fall into C minor as Gurnemanz addresses Parsifal: 'Oh Herr!'. So is confirmed the transformation of the foolish boy who killed the swan into the redeeming lord of the Grail.

The passage that I have here examined is not exceptional, and I have by no means exhausted the detail to which attention could be drawn. In its short span (its performance lasts barely four minutes) nothing happens – two characters stand still on the stage and sing in turn, while a third listens – and yet a great deal takes place. To Gurnemanz, Parsifal, as he tells his story, is revealed as the promised hero who will restore the Grail; by this revelation everything is changed, and in the opposite direction from Parsifal's apprehension of disaster in his 'verändert dünkt mich alles'. In this process, so swiftly set before us, not a word or a note is wasted. Every phrase – verbal and musical – tells, contributes to the precise, complicated unfolding of the drama, and to the ceaseless cumulative control of the audience's emotions. Wagner in the last act of his last work has perfected a minutely realized medium of expression, unique in the history of art. The lesson to be drawn, as we resume the speedier and less adequate pace of this synopsis, is that study of the sensitivity to nuance with which this work is put together is almost infinitely rewarding.

In a long narrative paragraph Gurnemanz now explains to Parsifal the present condition of the Grail brotherhood. To the forlorn music of the third-act prelude, which finds its most specific meaning in the connected suffering of Parsifal and the Grail, he tells of the distress to which the knights have been brought. With impassioned grief he recounts Amfortas's despair, which has led him, in his longing for death, to refuse to perform his office, so that the knights, deprived of their sacred food, wander about without courage or leader, their noble work lapsed. Dim echoes of the ceremonial music of the first act are heard. Gurnemanz concludes his account with the news of the death of Titurel; without the sight of the Grail, he was mortal as other men.

At this Parsifal utters a cry of despair:

> Und ich, ich bin's,
> der all dies Elend schuf!

> And I, it is I,
> who am the cause of all this misery!

This is *Mitleid* heightened by remorse; in an outburst of grief he mourns his folly and his blindness, his inability, though he is appointed to set all right, to find the last path that will lead him to his goal. This admission of his own guilt is the turning-point of the scene. After it, as he almost collapses with emotion and Kundry comes with water to revive him, the atmosphere changes to one of peace and gentleness. Kundry's action is accompanied by a plaintive theme, mild and sad, which was foreshadowed in the quieter moments of the scene between her and Parsifal in the second act. It has to do with the pathos of Kundry and with a reconciliation not then possible and now about to be achieved.

Gurnemanz, to a further development of the gentle music which has been heard only in the third act, replaces Kundry's bowl with water from the sacred spring to wash away the dust of Parsifal's journey. Kundry and Gurnemanz together remove Parsifal's armour and, as Kundry bathes Parsifal's feet, he watches her 'in silent wonder', the implication of this stage direction being that he now recognizes her. But he asks Gurnemanz to sprinkle his head; as he does so, the old man states the paradox implicit in all that has occurred since Parsifal's arrival: that he is both innocent and guilty, both the bearer of redemption and himself in need of redemption:

> Gesegnet sei, du Reiner, durch das Reine!
> So weiche jeder Schuld
> Bekümmernis von dir!

> May what is pure bless you, pure one!
> So may every sin be dissolved
> And suffering leave you.

The words are sung to a full statement of the new theme, thus associated with benediction and peace.

Kundry anoints Parsifal's feet and Parsifal, taking the phial of oil from her, hands it to Gurnemanz with the request that Titurel's comrade should anoint his head: 'dass heute noch als König er mich grüsse!' ('that today he may greet me also as King!'). This is Parsifal's second moment of triumph: drum-beats accompany the last four words and the theme associated with him expands to a victorious fanfare as Gurnemanz anoints his head and indeed greets him as king, praying to

Christ, who has suffered with him, to lift the last burden from his head. The words in which Gurnemanz addresses Christ, to a broadened transformation of the prophecy theme, show that in Wagner's mind Parsifal's saving destiny is closely associated with the redeeming power of Christ himself:

> Du — Reiner!
> Mitleidvoll Duldender,
> heiltatvoll Wissender!
> Wie des Erlösten Leiden du gelitten,
> die letzte Last entnimm nun seinem Haupt!

> Thou, pure one,
> compassionate sufferer,
> all-healing, all-knowing!
> As you have borne the sorrows of him who has been redeemed,
> take now the last burden from his head.

Gurnemanz's prayer ends to a resounding enunciation of the Grail theme which comes, for once, to a full close, followed by a pause.

The passage which succeeds this preparation of Parsifal for his sacred office is the true emotional climax of the opera. At a deeper level than the healing of Amfortas in the final scene, it sets forth reconciliation, forgiveness and the conquest of evil, these abstractions made concrete in the resolved relation between Kundry and Parsifal, and metaphorically expressed in the blossoming spring landscape which both words and music present.

Parsifal, with the words 'mein erstes Amt verricht' ich so' ('my first office I thus perform'), baptizes Kundry with water from the spring, telling her to believe in the Redeemer. To the steady theme suggesting faith, from the first-act prelude, Kundry bows her head and weeps bitterly. As the orchestra begins a gentle melody accompanied by soft string triplets, the scene always known as the Good Friday music, Parsifal looks with delight at the flowery fields. He compares their freshness to the sick craving of Klingsor's garden:

> Wie dünkt mich doch die Aue heut so schön!
> Wohl traf ich Wunderblumen an,
> die bis zum Haupte süchtig mich umrankten. . .

> How beautiful the meadows are to me today!
> Once I met with magic flowers
> that longingly twined about my head. . .

These words also suggest, of course, the contrast between the Kundry of the second act and Kundry as she now is. Gurnemanz explains the beauty of the morning: 'Das ist Karfreitags zauber, Herr!' ('That is the magic of Good Friday, Sire').

Parsifal suggests that, on this day of supreme sorrow, all that lives should rather weep: Kundry before him in tears seems to confirm his words, as does a surge of grief in the music. But Gurnemanz replies, to the reassertion of the Good Friday music, that it is the tears of repentant sinners which make the meadows flourish. The paragraph which follows seems to give a simple account of how the whole of creation rejoices on this day because man, saved by God's sacrifice and for the time being grateful and kind, will not injure nature or trample on the flowers. But Gurnemanz's words also illuminate what has taken place between Kundry and Parsifal. Of the created world he says:

> Ihn selbst am Kreuze kann sie nicht erschauen:
> da blickt sie zum erlösten Menschen auf;
> der fühlt sich frei von Sündenlast und Grauen.

> It cannot see the Saviour himself on the cross:
> it looks up to man redeemed,
> who feels freed from the burden of sin and fear.

This directly echoes his prayer that Parsifal should be freed from his last burden, and describes Parsifal as Kundry now sees him, redeemed. 'She looks up at him,' the stage direction says, 'in calm and serious entreaty.' What is more, the closing lines of Gurnemanz's speech refer again to the spring flowers, so unlike Klingsor's eternal temptress, and their newfound redemption:

> Das dankt dann alle Kreatur,
> was all da blüht und bald erstirbt,
> da die entsündigte Natur
> heut ihren Unschuldstag erwirbt.

> So all creation gives thanks,
> all that here blooms and soon dies,
> Nature from which sin has been lifted
> today wins its day of innocence.

Kundry has been released at last into the mortality of created beings; her penitence completed by the lifting of her curse from Parsifal, she will shortly die. Parsifal confirms her final salvation (and the full force of the metaphor) when, before the close of the Good Friday music, he quietly sings to her, remembering the magic garden where he last saw her:

Ich sah sie welken, die einst mir lachten:
ob heut sie nach Erlösung schmachten?
Auch deine Träne ward zum Segenstaue:
du weinest – sieh! es lacht die Aue!

I saw them wither who once laughed at me:
is it that today they long for redemption?
Your tears are also the dew of benediction:
you weep – look! how the meadows laugh.

(The two senses of 'laugh' here recall Wagner's remark about Kundry: 'She can only laugh and scream; she does not know true laughter.') As the music fades, Parsifal kisses Kundry on the forehead, his rescue of her finished and her mockery dissolved in tears.

The Grail bells are heard in the distance. The hour is come, Gurnemanz announces, and adds his last words in the opera, summing up all that he has been: 'Gestatte, Herr, dass dein Knecht dich geleite!' ('Allow, Sire, your servant to guide you'). He invests Parsifal with his mantle of the Grail knights; with Kundry, they begin to walk towards the castle as in the transformation in Act I but in the opposite direction. The music of this second transformation opens with Parsifal's theme as a sombre fanfare. This fades and yields to the slow crescendo of Titurel's funeral march as the Grail bells become louder and nearer. The three walking figures disappear from view and, after rocky vaults like those in Act I, the hall of the Grail is revealed, empty of the tables of Act I. Two processions of knights enter to the march, one carrying Titurel's coffin, and the other Amfortas on his litter preceded by the covered shrine of the Grail. As they converge, the processions sing alternate passages of a dirge which takes the form of questions, about the reasons for Titurel's death, from the knights carrying Amfortas, and answers from the knights carrying Titurel's body. These questions and answers, symmetrically matching, become shorter and shorter until the question: 'Wer wehrt' ihm des Grales Huld zu erschauen?' ('Who barred him from seeing the Grail's grace?') is answered: 'Den dort ihr geleitet, der sündige Hüter' ('He whom you bear here, the sinful guardian'). As the processions meet and set down their burdens the voices of the two groups join in angry and gloomy chorus: Amfortas will perform his office for the last time.

The effect of this convergence, and of the threatening repetition of the words 'Zum letzten Mal' ('For the last time'), is one of terrifying menace, as if the forces of retribution were finally closing on the wretched Amfortas. The knights' determination to see the Grail again, and thus to compel Amfortas to remain alive, seems no more than cruelty as Amfortas miserably sings:

> Williger nähm' ich von euch den Tod,
> der Sünde mildeste Sühne!

> More willingly would I suffer death from you,
> the gentlest atonement for sin!

When Titurel's coffin is opened, there is a cry from the knights. Wagner calls it a cry of woe, but the bullying posture of the knights suggests an accusing shout. Amfortas addresses his dead father in a long, halting prayer for his own death, to themes associated with his distress and the earlier history of the Grail. The knights have heard him plead also for the renewal of their life, but as his prayer ends they only crowd closer to him, fiercely ordering him to uncover the Grail: 'Du musst! Du musst!' ('You must!'). He leaps up wildly, pressed beyond endurance and crying that he will not. In frantic despair he tears the clothes from his wound and begs them to draw their swords and kill him.

This scene, in which Amfortas is tormented by his own knights like a sick animal rounded on by the pack, has a chilling horror quite different from Klingsor's Lucifer-like malice against the good. It is clear from the 1865 sketch that Wagner fully intended the brutal atmosphere he in fact created. 'Why this dreadful cruelty of casting him once again back into life?. . .Attempts at compulsion. Muttering and threats from the knights.' Though the scene does screw Amfortas's suffering to a new pitch of agony, it nevertheless seriously detracts from the picture of forlorn decay in the realm of the Grail which Gurnemanz has painted earlier in the act. It is a dislocation of the emotional unity of the work that the brotherhood all along represented by this kind old man should now behave in such a way.

Parsifal, who, with Gurnemanz and Kundry, has appeared unnoticed in the hall of the Grail, steps forward as Amfortas calls for the knights' weapons to kill him.

> Nur eine Waffe taugt:
> die Wunde schliesst
> der Speer nur, der sie schlug.

> One weapon only will serve:
> only the spear that inflicted it
> closes the wound.

Parsifal's intervention, accompanied by the final transformation of the music from darkness to light, restores not only Amfortas to health and the spear to its proper unity with the Grail, but also the psychological weight of the drama lost in the angry menace of the knights. The spear, the concrete object returned to its place and able to heal the wounded king, carries a complex load of symbolic meaning: it is the token of Amfortas's defeat and Parsifal's victory when confronted by identical temptation, identical experience. Thus it conveys the power of goodness to cancel evil by compassion, or, to retranslate 'durch Mitleid wissend', through enlightened suffering of the same fate. All of this Wagner summarized in the 1865 sketch in the words: 'Great is the magic power of him who desires; but greater still that of him who renounces', and it is indicated in Parsifal's ringing words as he raises the spear:

> Sei heil, entsündigt und gesühnt!
> Denn ich verwalte nun dein Amt.
> Gesegnet sei dein Leiden,
> das Mitleids höchste Kraft,
> und reinsten Wissens Macht
> dem zagen Toren gab!

> Be healed, absolved, and purged of sin!
> For I will now perform your office.
> Blessed be your suffering
> which gave compassion's highest power
> and the might of purest understanding
> to the timid fool!

Then, as his theme is heard in its last and most heroic form, he reaches the climax of his return to the Grail hall:

> Den heil'gen Speer —
> ich bring' ihn euch zurück!

> The holy spear —
> I bring it back to you!

In the 1865 sketch Amfortas, healed by the spear, was to uncover the Grail as before, and Titurel was to rise from his coffin miraculously restored to life. This, as Wagner no doubt realized, would have weakened the psychological force of all that has taken place in the drama by too simply restoring the situation as it was before Amfortas's fall. In the completed work Parsifal replaces Amfortas, forgiven but no longer king, and Titurel remains a corpse. As Parsifal turns to the Grail itself, three notes from the prophecy theme, the notes belonging to the words 'Mitleid wiss (end)', are heard on a single horn, and Parsifal sings: 'Nicht soll der mehr verschlossen sein' ('No more shall it be hidden'). The understanding his compassion has won can now reveal the Grail again to the world.

As he uncovers the shrine, the Grail gradually glows with increasing light and the music enters the long, shimmering conclusion to the work, the themes of order and light, faith and the power of the Grail, mingling and repeating in strings, woodwind, brass and harps. The knights and the unseen choir in the dome sing a final quiet chorus of celebration:

> Höchsten Heiles Wunder!
> Erlösung dem Erlöser!
>
> Highest wonder of salvation!
> Redemption to the redeemer!

The Grail, the symbol of the presence of Christ among men, has been saved from extinction. A white dove appears over Parsifal's head, Wolfram's dove which, every Good Friday, renews the power of the Grail — and Kundry sinks lifeless at his feet, her gaze still fixed on him. Amfortas and Gurnemanz kneel with the rest of the knights. On this tableau of reconciliation the curtain falls.

As with the libretti of all his mature works, Wagner regarded the text of *Parsifal* as a work of literature in its own right; he published it late in 1877 when he was still composing the music of the first act. In fact, of course, because in the creative process which produced the drama music and words were inseparably connected, the text can be read neither as a self-sufficient poem nor as a libretto written to be set to an as yet unconceived musical score. These words await completion not just in music but in the specific music of this one work of art, music already forming in Wagner's imagination as he wrote the text.

Since each of Wagner's scores — taking the *Ring* as a single work — has a powerful individuality which makes it easily identifiable from a few bars of music, it is not surprising that each text also has its own character. The *Stabreim* of the *Ring*, the short pregnant lines, irregularly rhymed, of *Tristan,* the much more leisurely lines and regular end-rhymes of *Die Meistersinger*: all of these contribute to the distinctive atmosphere of the drama concerned. The text of *Parsifal,* though in some passages denser in content than any of them, is nevertheless the most relaxed in form, the least self-consciously literary, the most flexibly adapted to the demands of the musical drama. Rhyme, as we have seen, is used from time to time, for purposes of emphasis and contrast; its use is inconsistent enough for its effect to be almost always striking. In the first scene of the third act, for example, there is no rhyme at all until the climax of Parsifal's account of his return of the spear, which ends with two rhymed pairs of lines. Gurnemanz's long account of the Grail's plight is unrhymed: Parsifal's lament over his own guilt ends, again, with four rhymed lines. At the anointing, Parsifal's words are rhymed while Gurnemanz's prayer is not; in contrast, Parsifal's lines on the flowery meadows and on the grief of Good Friday are unrhymed, so as to give more weight to the elaborate rhyme-scheme of Gurnemanz's meditation on the meaning of Good Friday. The scene closes with Parsifal's four lines to Kundry which consist of two regularly scanned and rhymed couplets. It is significant, also, that in the first Grail scene both the knights' utterances and Amfortas's lament are strongly rhymed, whereas in the disarray and despair of the second Grail scene there is almost no rhyme until the three resounding couplets with which Parsifal restores the spear to the Grail.

But the essential characteristic of the text of *Parsifal* is neither its flexible use of rhyme nor its diction, which is less archaic and less stylized than in Wagner's other libretti. What most of all distinguishes these words from all their predecessors is the level of abstraction they attain and the precision with which, on that level, they are used. Wagner does not here leave us in the condition of doubt (fertile in conflicting theory) which surrounds the complex fate of Wotan, Tristan and even Sachs. Kundry, Amfortas and Parsifal undergo experiences of which the meaning is abstract, spiritual and not at all simple, but Wagner tells us precisely what that meaning is. The words specify significances which are at a distant remove from what may be conveyed either by music or by visible action on the stage. The second-act scene between Kundry and Parsifal, for example, without detailed comprehension of the words, looks and sounds only like a seduction resisted at some length. What is really afoot is made clear – and crystal clear – in Parsifal's several descriptions of Kundry's plight and his own identification with Amfortas. Similarly Gurnemanz, setting forth the particular holiness of Good Friday, expresses an idea which, though full of the emotion of the scene before us and the encompassing music, can be made exact only in words.

In these and many other passages in *Parsifal* Wagner leaves the concrete images of the realm of myth and enters the realm of theology, the realm of transforming explanation. A moment's comparison of Siegfried and Parsifal, both fearless innocents who attain adulthood through the discovery of desire and supplant the damaged hero who awaits them, shows that they inhabit different worlds. The difference is established in the words they use and the words that are used about them.

The text of *Parsifal*, nevertheless, also has moments of pure drama, as simple and as compact with emotional force as anything in Wagner. To take only one example, Parsifal's first words in the third act: 'Heil mir, dass ich dich wiederfinde!', not only echo Gurnemanz's greeting, just offered without recognition, but his own parting words to Kundry in Act II: 'Du weisst, wo du mich wiederfinden kannst!' They are surrounded by Gurnemanz's questions, 'Bist du verirrt, und soll ich dich weisen?', 'Welche Pfade fand er?', and then, 'Wie kamst du heut? Woher?', so that when Parsifal speaks for the second time his desolate answer fulfils a powerfully built-up expectation: 'Der Irrnis und der Leiden Pfade kam ich'. There is also a hint of the first-act prescription that the Grail can be discovered only by those who come 'auf Pfaden die kein Sünder findet'. This kind of subtlety in the making of a dramatic point has been noticed several times in the above synopsis.

Wagner wrote the text of *Parsifal* in one month and five days (14 March – 19 April 1877). He had been writing the words for his own operas for more than forty years; he had been meditating this subject for more than thirty. The text he produced was the work of a consummate master: the shape of scenes, the parallels between scenes, the placing of climaxes, the brevity of some utterances and the expansiveness of others, are all handled with a sure dramatic skill which left the composer in him a libretto to set that needed not a single substantial alteration. But more remarkable still was the creative certainty which allowed him to write into the actual substance of his text an extra-dramatic and extra-musical interpretation, clear and precise, which forcibly channels and directs the audience's response to both music and drama. It is this direction, this definition of meaning, which, more than the subject-matter of the work, makes *Parsifal* such an odd artistic creation; for here Wagner reaches the extreme point of the undertaking, never before attempted and peculiar to himself, which occupied him all his life: the definition of particular significance by the mutual *limitation* of words and music. The critic of *Parsifal* is compelled to begin his account not with an enquiry into what the work may or may not be about, but with a discussion of its self-declared content. This necessity has, as we shall see, raised more critical problems than it has solved.

3 *The music*

BY ARNOLD WHITTALL

> How easy it would be if I could just write arias and duets! Now every-
> thing has to be a little musical portrait, but it must not interrupt the
> flow.
>
> From Cosima Wagner's diary, 18 July 1871

> This music which is in perpetual *evolution* is probably the most highly
> personal musical invention of Wagner – it places the emphasis for the
> first time on uncertainty, on indetermination. It represents a rejection
> of immutability, an aversion to definitiveness in musical phrases as long
> as they have not exhausted their potential for evolution and renewal.
>
> Pierre Boulez on *Parsifal*, notes accompanying DG 2713 004

I

In the simplest, most immediate sense the opening of *Parsifal* demonstrates the primacy of theme: it is a monody which shuns regular pulsa-
tion. It is not, however, monochrome: a single clarinet and bassoon
double violins and cellos (Wagner asks for the first player from each desk
only) and the alto oboe (cor anglais) adds a new timbre to the line
during its most expressive central phrase (see ex. 1).

ex. 1

To bow to tradition and call this melody the 'Love Feast' theme is
perhaps not totally foolish, since it follows up a cue of the composer's.
But the extent to which words can adequately translate the expressive
quality and dramatic significance of themes and motives is bound to
vary very greatly, not only according to the changing contexts in which

61

3 Wieland Wagner's set for the Magic Garden, Act II Scene 2; Bayreuth 1951—5

the material occurs, but also according to the predispositions of each individual listener. Like all Wagner's more developed thematic ideas, this one is more important for its musico-dramatic potential than for its illustrative precision. Music communicates most immediately and generally through the atmosphere its themes and textures create, and it is not the job of the analyst to interfere in this direct contact between composer and listener: his prime concern is with structure, not translatable meaning. Nevertheless, through description and interpretation of the formal principles and technical procedures with which those themes and motives are presented and manipulated, the analyst can provide a foundation, a background against which the individual interpretation of the dramatic significance of thematic components may be placed. And, if human, the analyst can rarely exclude all discussion of dramatic meaning from his technical commentary.

The character of this initial theme is crucial to the style of *Parsifal*, and the contained richness of the sound, as well as the number of shorter motives which comprise it, presage thematic processes of great intensity. Yet before a thematic process as such begins there is a harmonized repetition of the theme which draws attention to its only slightly disturbed diatonicism. The harmonization also renders the basic metre more explicit, and the instrumentation establishes that the richness of the surrounding figuration, if not itself strictly speaking 'thematic', contributes substantially to to the essential character of a theme or motive.

A commentary on *Parsifal* concerned principally with motives would doubtless be able to present a formidably lengthy list of statements, derivations and transformations, in which interest would centre not only on the composer's promptness in responding to the cues implanted in his own text, but also on the commentator's ingenuity in noting possible connections. Yet it is not the mere presence of thematic material, whether obviously or deviously derived from a particular *Gestalt* or not, which is important, so much as the relationship of the musical and dramatic character of that material to the total context in which it appears. Carl Dahlhaus has observed that

in greatly simplified terms, the use of musical motives in *Parsifal* is governed by the contrast of chromaticism and diatonicism [a contrast that can only be fully realised when harmony as well as melody is involved]: the chromaticism that conveys the deceptions of Klingsor's kingdom also expresses the anguish of Amfortas, while the expressive range of the diatonicism reaches from the naive simplicity of Parsifal's motive to the sublimity of the Grail theme.[1]

In Wagner's style, however, diatonic motives have a greater potential for becoming chromatic than chromatic ones have for becoming diatonic, and it follows that diatonicism is always more likely to dissolve into chromaticism than chromaticism is to resolve into diatonicism. Moreover, because of the flexibility with which diatonic and chromatic elements can interact, the context around a particular motive will never be a foregone conclusion. Wagner's genius lay not in providing a series of separate, well-characterized 'symphonic poems' around the motives appropriate to each stage in the story, but in composing a succession of episodes linked by a fusion of harmonic process and motivic correspondence: in not interrupting 'the flow'. Nor is 'flow' a mere matter of avoiding the regular occurrence of strong cadences, but of perfecting that progressive mutability of theme and tonal relation which are at the heart of Wagner's musico-dramatic technique. Harmony is not the passive servant of melody: the two interact to generate the evolving musical structure of the drama. Hence the problems consequent on attempting too rigid or monolithic an interpretation of Wagner's fundamental harmonic procedures.

These procedures, in essence, involve the creation of a process whereby relatively short passages of pure diatonicism, cadentially defined, coherently co-exist and interact with prolonged passages of expanded tonality and of chromatic flux. In the passages of expanded tonality a tonic chord may be established and cadentially confirmed, but highly chromatic expansions will occur between the principal points of emphasis on that tonic. In the passages of chromatic flux, cadential progressions may also occur, but they are unlikely to establish tonics for diatonic prolongation or chromatic expansion. Opinions may well vary as to whether a particular passage represents expanded tonality or chromatic flux, but if a chord seems sufficiently well established to reduce chromatic elements to an ornamental role, then it can acquire the quality of a tonic even if diatonic progressions are minimal. Such tonics may be highly unstable, but they are still the least unstable element in contexts where the motion is highly contrapuntal in character.

Dahlhaus has noted the appropriateness of Schoenberg's terms 'floating' or 'roving' tonality for passages in Wagner where the tonality is so ambiguous as to admit of at least two different interpretations, or where it seems to be suspended altogether.[2] Of 'atonality', save on the smallest scale, there is little sign: even in as radically expressionistic a passage as Kundry's account of laughing in the face of Christ, with its emphasis on various seventh chords, an underlying tonal centre of B can be detected, and the introduction to Act III undeniably alludes to tonal forces, even if they are of a rather special kind.

At various points in *Parsifal* it is possible to feel that a tonality is present and identifiable through emphasis on its dominant note or chord, even if the tonic itself is absent. Whether or not a dominant is 'truly' a dominant if its tonic is not actually present is a large theoretical issue. But if a dominant does not actually function as such, to the extent of preparing the assertion of its tonic, it is more likely to be the agent of floating than of expanded tonality. The presence of an un-resolving dominant may make awareness of the absence of the ap-propriate tonic a factor in one's experience of the work, but such a dominant can hardly be held automatically to imply the actual presence, still less the function, of a tonic: it is the absence of resolution which is the crucial factor, not its implied presence.

The fundamental importance of tonality in *Parsifal,* and the evident persistence of certain types of tonal relationships, notably the familiar nineteenth-century emphasis on chords and keys a third apart to open up broader perspectives than those provided by emphasis on dominant and subdominant relations, seem to invite the proposal of some grand theory, not merely of tonal *usage,* but of tonal *unity. Parsifal* certainly coheres around tonal as well as thematic recurrences, and most of the principal tonal centres are found on the minor or major third axes around A flat. Yet it is still difficult to regard the A flat major in which the work beings and ends, and which occurs from time to time during its course, as performing the kind of pivotal function that the tonic key of a symphonic structure performs: such 'monotonality' is as impracticable a concept in a music drama as it is in a number opera. Attempts to relate the tonal and harmonic organisation of *Parsifal* to procedures more specific and systematic than those of expanded or floating tonality are as unwise as attempts to discuss its form solely in terms of AAB and ABA. Yet it can be argued that the importance of large-scale third relations is paralleled by the special prominence of powerfully expressive chords constructed from three minor thirds (the diminished seventh); from two minor thirds and one major (a 'secondary' seventh, for example D, F, A flat, C: the 'Tristan' chord is of this basic type); or from some other, more complex 'dominant-quality' chords. The importance of such chords in *Parsifal* can scarcely be disputed, and some association between them and large-scale tonal relationships, such as those between A flat, B and D in all three acts, can therefore be sensed and described. Of course, the consistent employment of minor third and tritone relations, in chords, progressions and juxtaposed tonal areas, tends to break down the hierarchic structure of the tonal system into something directed more towards symmetrical division of the octave. Such a breakdown is essentially a post-Wagnerian phenomenon, however, and what unifies Wagner's harmonic practice in all his music dramas, most fundamentally, is the structural precedence that the major and minor triad still ultimately has over the other less stable, highly expressive harmonic constructs. Increasing tension may be sensed between forces making for hierarchy and forces making for symmetry, just as there is heightened tension between dissonances and consonances when the former do not immediately resolve onto the latter. But Wagner's flexible, evolving harmonic process still favours the dissolution of dissonance, even though traditional diatonic progressions may occur relatively rarely.

The primary role of tonal relations in *Parsifal* is to ensure an evolving musical continuity within which the motives can function both symbolically and structurally. There is certainly some association between themes and the keys or tonal areas in which they appear, but the work does not demonstrate a rigid, all-inclusive system of tonal relations based on such associations, still less some rigid scheme of tonal symbolism which embraces every twist and turn of tonal motion. If we have an ear for such things, the fact that A flat major is used for the blandishments of the Flower Maidens as well as for the knights of the Grail will reinforce the structural significance of that key without necessarily suggesting that the two groups of individuals are meant to be seen as symbolically or actually related.

With flexibility predominant in the harmonic and tonal sphere, it remains to note the importance of fluctuating tempos. Pierre Boulez has remarked that the tempo tends to be 'very fluctuating in what I would call the recitatives – the action; it becomes more fixed and stabilized in the reflective passages, the commentary'.[3] So no would-be 'complete' analysis of *Parsifal* can ignore the interaction between tonality and tempo as the means whereby the interaction between text and music is most comprehensively articulated.

II

The first two motives within the opening theme of the Prelude to Act I of *Parsifal* relate to triads of A flat major and C minor, while the final motive, when harmonized, progresses back towards a triad of A flat. This is the first evidence of third-relations, and the Prelude as a whole can certainly be felt to encapsulate those processes of the work which relate to such progressions, and to expansions of essentially diatonic, cadentially established tonalities. There is obviously the greatest difference between the kind of small-scale shift from A flat to C and back again within the initial thematic statement, amounting to no more than a slight chromatic expansion (the D natural passing-note) of the basic A flat, and large-scale motions in which each new tonic may be cadentially established and extended. But the principle laid down in the Prelude, and its structural completion in the early bars of Act I, is of eventual closure, of diatonic resolution.

The small and large-scale expansions of the Prelude are the agents of a clear formal outline, comprising four principal sections. First, the initial statement, in monodic and harmonized forms, presents a binary expansion and clarification of the A flat major triad, and ultimately, through cadential preparation and resolution, of the A flat major tonality. The second section (from bar 20) consists of a slightly modified restatement of that paragraph, intensified by tonal transposition onto C minor (the initial third-relation raised to a higher level of structure); this results in two small-scale appearances of an E minor triad as the agent of tonal expansion. The third section of the Prelude (from bar 39) provides a return to, and emphasis on, the original tonal area of A flat major, but with new material (the Grail and Faith motives) and much more elaborate expansions which match the sequential treatment of the material, as well as its development by the striking alteration of rhythmic values. The section returns to A flat major, but its internal expansions are considerably more extreme than those of its two predecessors. In particular, the dramatic assertion of G flat major and D major harmony after the first tonic to dominant motion opens up the prospect of a greater extension of the movement by thirds, and this actually occurs in the final section of the Prelude. Before leaving the third section, however, it is worth noting that the first statements of the Faith motive (bars 44-55) form one of the few passages from Wagner to be discussed by an adherent of Heinrich Schenker's theories of tonal structure.[4] These theories, with their emphasis on the linear projection or prolongation of fundamental harmonic elements and on the basic function of progressions from tonic to dominant and back to tonic, remain the most important and satisfying for the (relatively) small-scale instrumental forms found in sonata and symphony. But Schenker, like Schoenberg after him, believed that Wagner's expansion — or, in Schenker's view, destruction — of traditional tonal structures was provoked primarily by extra-musical influences, the demands of dramatic subject and text. So Adèle Katz argues that such 'extra-musical effects' as the restatements of the Faith motive in G flat and D 'are achieved at the sacrifice of the structural coherence'. Katz effectively demonstrates that Wagner's technique is radically different from that of the upholders of the tonal symphonic tradition so beloved of Schenkerians, and culminating in Brahms: but in claiming incoherence for such a small passage unrelated to the whole, she does not convince.

The fourth and final section of the Prelude (from bar 78) develops the initial theme, but 'development' is as much a matter of tonal process as of purely thematic — intervallic and rhythmic — manipulation. The tonal and thematic cannot be separated, not least when such importance is attached to small-scale sequential transpositions, and both combine to create the first substantial point of closure in the work, for which only the dominant preparation takes place within the Prelude itself. It eventually resolves onto the tonic of A flat when the Grail motive returns as frame to a new A flat major paragraph, at Gurnemanz's 'so wacht doch mindest am Morgen'.

Even before the main action begins, with Gurnemanz rousing the sleeping squires, there is a brief example of the kind of 'recitative' which is often separated sharply from more characteristic textures in commentaries on the work (see ex. 2). Yet even in phrases which aspire to no great lyric heights, and appear to fit themselves into the prevailing motivic material provided by the orchestra, principles of organization and unification can be detected. Gurnemanz's first line outlines an E

ex. 2

He! Ho! Wald-hü-ter ihr! Schlaf-hü-ter mit-sam-men! so wacht doch min-dest am

Mor - gen!

flat triad, ascending in echo of the first three notes of the Prelude's first theme, while the second line (marked a1 in ex. 2) extends and decorates the descent which ends the first. The third line — 'so wacht doch mindest am Morgen' — can be regarded as a variant of the first, or of the first two combined, still basically prolonging the dominant note, since this is what the accompaniment decrees. Clearly, the verbal parallel between 'Waldhüter ihr' and 'Schlafhüter mitsammen' has suggested a musical parallel, with a greater degree of emphasis on 'Schlaf-' than on

'Wald-'. Yet, as complement as much as continuation, 'so wacht doch mindest am Morgen' could have been set in a much more contrasted way without compromising its dramatic significance. Clearly, Wagner will not invariably use verbal parallels as justifications for musical ones, nor will the absence of the former preclude the use of the latter. And even in phrases like these, where the thematic content is rudimentary and there is no accompaniment to speak of, a process or relationship by extension and expansion is evident, which is of the greatest importance in a work where freedom is never confused with randomness. I would not be so incautious as to claim that such connections are all-pervading, or that they were consciously contrived by Wagner, but Gurnemanz's next paragraph — 'Jetzt auf, ihr Knaben!' — begins with a group of statements in which motion between high and low B naturals provides a framework for small-scale variation.

Act I contains only one change of actual location, but a much larger number of different character groupings. Of the principals, only Gurnemanz is not represented by a motive or motives: and it follows that his narrations, which are more significant for what they tell us about others than for what they tell us about him, can the more effectively deal with ideas and events involving the more active characters.

As the action begins in earnest, with Gurnemanz addressing the squires, the characteristically ambiguous tonal processes and fluctuating tempos of the work are revealed for the first time. During the preparation for Amfortas's arrival, which includes the first references to the Prophecy motive (at 'Toren wir') certain tonal tendencies can be identified, but these are not confirmed by the kind of ample cadential progressions which have marked the music up to this point. The main point of articulation — after 'Befahl er eifrig uns das Bad' — is an A which could function as the dominant of D minor, but that resolution will not take place in any really decisive fashion until the moment before Parsifal's actual entrance.

Instability increases with Kundry's precipitate appearance. The sudden A flats after 'Sorgt für das Bad!' could presage a rapid recovery of the Prelude's tonality, but this note is present now not as a tonic, nor even as the root of a triad, but as part of a shifting complex of chromatic chords based first on D and then, when the F-B tritone is 'translated' into E sharp-B, preparing an F sharp in the bass with the kind of aggregate above it which could resolve through a conventional dominant onto a B minor tonic, but does not in fact do so.

When Amfortas's procession enters, to the 'weighty' 3/2 which Wagner wanted 'so as to make the words of Gurnemanz fit' (Cosima

Wagner's Diary, 10 October 1877), his harmony is more stable than Kundry's because his motive is more sustained, but there is still no diatonic cadence to root the music unambiguously. An incidental cadence onto D flat in Gurnemanz's introductory paragraph – 'des siegreichsten Geschlechtes Herrn' – may help to prepare the much stronger resolution into G flat major at the end of Amfortas's own first paragraph – at 'die Schmerzensnacht wird helle'. But both are at once abandoned, and the general orientation has in any case been very different – towards D minor, B flat major and F major, the last with the plain dominant preparation which precedes the ironic eleven-crotchet silence at 'Ein wenig Rast'.

This technique, whereby the most explicit diatonic cadences are placed in a prevailingly contradictory, ambiguous context, shows the dramatic appropriateness of the diatonic/chromatic interaction very strongly indeed. When the only keys to be realized cadentially are incidental ones the music can acquire not merely a restless but a deeply poignant quality: Amfortas comes very close to the healing purity of a calm, cadentially confirmed B flat major, and the orchestration, with its lulling ostinati in the four horns, seems on the verge of a paradisal release, but this ultimate resolution is denied him. He must continue to suffer.

Although the first Amfortas episode is more triadic (and therefore, in Wagnerian terms, more positively ambiguous) than the first Kundry episode, they both form a firm contrast to the enclosed expansions of the Prelude. It is clear that Wagner's essential musico-dramatic technique is not merely a matter of preparing and then evading cadences, but an almost ironic reversal of traditional cadential function. The fewer the points of diatonic cadential resolution, the greater their structural significance might appear to be. But if some of these resolutions are outside the prevailing implied tonality, as with the D flat and G flat cadences during the first Amfortas episode, they resolve nothing: they rather enhance the prevailing instability, and create an even stronger contrast with the truly structural cadences which *do* confirm prevailing tonal tendencies.

Gurnemanz's long narration, which follows Amfortas's departure, confirms this more active ambiguity. Dramatically, it has a clear goal, the appearance of Parsifal. Musically, its succession of rich motivic complexes articulates a series of tonal areas, many approached and briefly defined in passing: others, like the initial E minor, more firmly established; but there is no single, over-riding tonic, whatever the larger-scale implications of, for example, the two cadences onto E flat at 'verlor'nen Speer!' and 'Zaub'rer zu beheeren?'. Motives are rarely absent, but Wagner is careful not to employ them so obviously or unremittingly that their presence becomes wearisome. For example, at the very outset – 'Wann alles ratlos steht' – the prevailing Kundry material is suppressed for a few bars, if only because it might propel the music forward at too fast a pace. But it returns at 'doch, wann's in Gefahr', and thereafter the narration is dominated by motivic processes.

The way in which elements from different motives can be brought together within a harmonic orbit supporting the prevailing D minor orientation is shown in example 3. Gurnemanz is describing how Kundry serves the knights: the opening of the Prelude's first theme on A minor (see A in ex. 3) leads through a hint of the Prophecy motive whose presence is scarcely required by the text (see B in ex. 3) to a version of the Faith motive (see C in ex. 3) and a fragment of Kundry's material (see D in ex. 3) at 'dienet uns'. Later, at 'dereinst des Heilands

ex. 3 (accompaniment reduced)

Parsifal

selige Boten', a more expansive thematic paragraph is framed by parallel statements of the Grail theme prolonging the triads of G flat and F sharp respectively. The material here is drawn from example 1 and a new derivative of the Faith motive, associated with Titurel and the knights as guardians of the Spear and Grail (see ex. 4). But two modified statement of the Grail theme, the first only a fragment, punctuate the paragraph and illustrate with particular clarity the kind of modifications which Wagner employed to ensure comprehension and continuity: and the 'exact' repetition of the Grail theme, at the end, is differently orchestrated.

ex. 4

This is the last of Wagner's great narrations, and it accumulates an atmosphere of solemn exaltation as Gurnemanz recounts the story of Titurel, Klingsor and Amfortas. It is, of course, rather more an observer's than a participant's tale, and lacks some of the supreme cumulative power of Wotan's great monologue in Act II of *Die Walküre* or of Tristan's in Act III of *Tristan und Isolde*. Even so, its concentrated motivic working shows that the new, reflective tone of the *Bühnen-weihfestspiel* was not achieved at the cost of thinning down a musico-dramatic technique evolved for very different subjects, but rather of refining it.

The association of motive with tonal area gives the end of the narration a particular power: at 'ein sel'ger Schimmer' the A flat of the Grail, having moved into the closely related key of D flat, switches suddenly onto the dominant of D for the first cadentially confirmed statement of the Prophecy motive. This concentration on the two aspects of the drama which will ultimately be brought together is the more apt considering the sheer range of Gurnemanz's narration, which has reached as far into the musical future of the work as a hint of the Flower Maidens' A flat at 'wen er verlockt'. It also suggests rather strongly that the tonal centres of A flat and D are indeed associates rather than opponents. (The final stages of Parsifal's address to the knights near the end of Act III will move from a grand D major climax to a resolution in A flat major.)

On his first appearance, Parsifal is presented musically as a carefree huntsman — hence the fanfare motive, indicating Siegfried-like qualities. The action here is very fluid, and the strongest cadence is the very plain and conventional C minor resolution at Gurnemanz's 'Unerhörtes Werk'. Its main effect is to ensure a return to a more leisurely pace. It does not have much immediate influence on the tonal direction of the music, but it is the first clear emphasis since the Prelude on the tonic note which will frame a large part of the later stages of the act, and eventually end it. What is also clear is that the 'carefree', but never strongly supported B flat major area in which Parsifal himself first appears — it will be transformed into an intensely ambiguous B flat minor at the beginning of Act III — disintegrates further as he is faced with unanswerable questions. Wagner informed Cosima that he had 'concocted a fine *mélange* for the esquires as they remove the dead swan: Amfortas's theme, Herzeleide's theme, and the swan motive from *Lohengrin'* (Diary, 5 December 1877). But chromaticism reaches its greatest concentration in Kundry's final broken utterances, after her first undermining of Parsifal's boyish self-assurance; then the last note of a wandering bass clarinet line — an A — is taken up as the starting point for the final, much more triadic stage of the scene. The triads are appropriate if only because Gurnemanz's benign mood has been restored, but they do not betoken any greater diatonic stability: rather, a more intense balance between consonant harmonic vocabulary and floating tonal succession.

The post-Schenkerian analyst Felix Salzer has taken the 78-bar passage beginning at Gurnemanz's 'Vom Bade kehrt' and extending to the entrance of the bells to illustrate 'a prolongation of exceptional expansion', with the conclusion, 'one cannot help marvelling at the incredible correlation between drama and music'.[5] The fact that, from the climax of the transformation music – the principal cadence is at Gurnemanz's parenthetical 'welch' Wissen dir auch mag beschieden sein' – to the last three hushed chords, the music of Act I is framed by pure C major does not make it possible to regard it all as being *in* C major, of course. But with this relatively decisive degree of framing stability, there is also a sense of a more determined use of third-relations around C, with E (in Amfortas's 'aria'), A flat (during the Celebration when the music of the Prelude returns), and E flat (for the Recession) particularly prominent.

The mode of expression of the knights is in sharp contrast to that of Amfortas, and their music, part chorale, part marching-song, requires a plainer harmonic vocabulary and simpler rhythms. The apparent plainness of their melodic material may discourage motivic scrutiny, but the relationship between the initial descending line at 'Zum letzten Liebesmahle' and the Faith motive should not be overlooked: nor the connection between the central segment of example 1 and the line at 'der Labung darf er nah'n' (see ex. 5). Later, the first stanza of the hymn 'Nehmet von Brot' provides a rare example in *Parsifal* of purely diatonic music (save for one chromatic passing-note).

ex. 5

Chorus of Knights

Zum letz-ten Lie-bes-mah – – le   der La – – bung darf er nah'n.

The greatest contrast to the relative diatonic stability of the processional and celebratory music is, obviously, provided by Amfortas's anguished lament. This begins in a curiously formal manner, with a recitative cadence onto a tonic – 'zu diesem Amt verdammt zu sein' – and a four-bar preliminary statement of his first melodic phrase preceded by a bar of syncopated E minor harmony. This beginning, like that of Gurnemanz's earlier narration, which also starts in E minor, may of course be intentionally 'unpromising' and plain, simply to prepare the ground for some highly complex and concentrated motivic development. Tonally, the music does not tend wholly towards the sharp side, but the cadences on A minor (at 'O, Strafe!') and E minor (at 'der Göttliche weint') prepare most decisively for the concluding confirmation of D with the return of the Prophecy theme in its cadencing form. When Prophecy and Grail were juxtaposed at the end of Gurnemanz's narration, the D of the Prophecy motive came second, and was immediately swept aside. Now the Grail's A flat comes second, and after Titurel's 'enthüllet den Gral!' a long dominant preparation precedes the return of the Prelude's elaboration of its opening theme. In places Wagner sustains tension by bringing A flat and C major into close proximity and therefore keeping open the possibility that the act might end in the key in which it starts: the treatment of the Grail motive immediately after Titurel's final phrase, 'wie hell grüsst uns heute der Herr', and the equivalent point in the recessional music, where the return of the bells ensures a degree of stability for C major, are examples. The textural, spatial and timbral features of this scene could be material for an extended essay in themselves, but it is at least worth noting that differentiation of tone-colours can be as crucial a feature as the celebrated blending for which Wagner is so often praised. After the strings, led by violas, have so vividly characterized Parsifal's goose-like demeanour, the widely-spaced C major chords which close the act are sustained by woodwind and brass only, with a quiet *pizzicato* chord from the strings and the penultimate bell-stroke marking the first beat of the final bar.

III

Act I of *Parsifal* is as much concerned with the past as with the present. It develops through time, space and place, so it is appropriate that, by the end, C major, the second most stable tonal area after the Prelude's A flat, should give that A flat a new perspective. The continuity provided by particularly clear and prominent use of familiar motives in the later stages of the act is therefore offset – balanced, to a degree – by the new tonal environment in which they are placed. But Act II is more concentrated, dealing essentially with the preparation and enactment of a single event, the 'trial' of Parsifal himself. It is also the only act in all Wagner's music dramas to begin and end in the same key — unless we consider that Act I of *Tristan und Isolde* begins at the end of the Prelude. The music of Act II is also more uniform than that of Act I, the predominant motives and harmonic contexts ensuring a more consistent level of chromaticism. It could be argued that there are only five points — or areas — of strong cadential confirmation of a tonality in its entire length, and since these identify the keys of B minor, E flat major, A flat major, G major and B minor again, major-minor third relations around B are consistently in evidence.

The tonalities each occur in connection with important issues or events: B minor with Klingsor's demonic self-assertion, E flat with Parsifal's initial appearance as described by Klingsor ('Sie weichen! Sie fliehen!'), A flat with the Flower Maidens' seductive strains (the most diatonic music in Act II), G major with Kundry's more artful attempts to undermine the hero's chastity, and B minor with Klingsor's defeat. But they and their more significant subsidiaries provide no more than the most basic framework or scaffolding upon which the motivic process can be projected, and within which the large areas of floating tonality can be introduced: above all, the central events of the act, the kiss and Parsifal's reaction, call for intense chromaticism, not for triadic cadential progressions, however temporarily secure.

In Act I the least triadic, most dissonant passages were relatively incidental: those centering on Kundry, where Klingsor is discussed by Gurnemanz, and in which Amfortas's anguish is revealed as the direct result of contact with these evil forces. Now Parsifal's achievement of self-realization in Act II, prepared by a use of the Tristan chord at the word 'Kuss'[6] which is surely as deliberate as the reference to *Lohengrin* for the dying swan in Act I (see ex. 6), results not in an access of

ex. 6

diatonic purity in which even the mildly unstable Prophecy motive is drained of its tension, but in a positive passionate chromaticism which initially outdoes in its avoidance of cadential confirmations the more 'decadent' material of Kundry or Klingsor. Of course, what Parsifal has discovered at this stage gives him no cause for serenity, and the 'new man' needs no new motives, simply a new relationship with the old ones. Indeed, the process goes beyond relationship into identification. Parsifal's memory of Amfortas's lament and the Grail ceremony is so acute, so far beyond that of a merely compassionate observer, that his own motives do not appear at all. During the first stage, from 'Amfortas! Die Wunde!' to 'in sündigem Verlangen!' the material is that of Amfortas, Kundry and the anguished central segment of example 1, the chromaticism so intense that a climactic F minor third at 'nun blutet sie in mir!' is of no structural significance whatever. The main point of focus is the chord of superimposed thirds which launches the entire episode (E, G, B flat, D flat, F) and the modified version of it at 'Nein! Nein! Nicht die Wunde ist es' (E, G, B flat, D). The second stage, from 'Es starrt der Blick' to 'Wie büss ich, Sünder, meine Schuld?' is introduced by two chromatically distorted versions of the Grail theme (see ex. 7) and continues with all three elements of example 1, derivations of the third being given special prominence.

ex. 7 (reduction; voice omitted)

Yet in spite of the increase in triadic harmony the music remains suspended around points of focus which are not approached distonically and soon disintegrate. The two main points of focus are provided by the opening of example 1: first, a version beginning in C minor like the second statement of the Act I Prelude dissolves into sequential treatment of its final segment; second, a version in A flat minor, at 'Erlöse, rette mich', seems likely to achieve greater stability until the dominant harmony at 'laut mir in die Seele' moves chromatically rather than diatonically, and the harmony begins to drift back towards G major or B minor, both keys suggesting that Kundry's spell has yet to be completely dispersed.

In Act II of *Siegfried*, Wagner had brilliantly succeeded in depicting his hero's sudden attainment of maturity after the death of Fafner and the Woodbird's warning. The dialogues which dominate the rest of that work – with Mime, the Wanderer and Brünnhilde – enable Siegfried to assert a power which has so far been evident in a relatively immature manner. The change which comes over Parsifal at the centre of Act II is musically more difficult to carry through because the character has so far been less fully developed. In *Tannhäuser* there is also a crisis for the central character at the mid-point of the drama, but there he is turned into the more conventional romantic figure of the outcast; and Lohengrin's later moment of truth, when he fails to prevent Elsa from asking the forbidden question, leaves him with the role of outcast also. But the passions and duties which so become Wagner's more tragic heroes, and which inspire such sublime music, have no place in *Parsifal*. In his earlier works, Wagner had shown mastery of the essentially romantic, passionate arguments between male and female which are the opposite of vehement declarations of love, and which in various ways chart progression from shared feeling to desperate disillusionment. But Parsifal and Kundry have not really shared anything, in spite of her knowledge of his past, which so disturbed him in Act I; and so they tend to react to each other rhetorically in music which seeks energy and forcefulness through a diffusion of thematic character and reduction in rhythmic elaboration which in places is distinctly incongruous. From the plain interrupted cadence at Parsifal's 'Verderberin! Weiche von mir!' the contrast between hints of the composer's earlier manner and reassertions of the late style (most obviously at Kundry's 'Ich sah Ihn') is disturbing, and a jarring motivic insertion – the Faith theme at 'des einz'gen Heiles wahren Quell?' – reinforces one's feeling that the music here is not wholly focused in style. Full vitality and sense of direction are recovered at the point where the final, extended B minor area is established – Parsifal's 'zeigest du zu Amfortas mir den Weg'. There are two principal motions towards the third-relative D during this section: an implied perfect cadence in D minor, with the tonic note only in the voice, at Kundry's 'und des Weges sollst du geleitet sein', and the brief vision of D major when Klingsor throws the spear. But even though a pure B minor tonic triad is reserved for the very end of the act a strong framework of expanded tonality is provided which not only confirms the third-related preoccupations of the work as a whole, but provides a suitable context for the prolonged passages of less stable, floating tonality within the act.

IV

Acts I and II of *Parsifal* both begin and end with cadentially confirmed areas of expanded tonality, but the orchestral introduction to Act III, though oriented around B flat minor, floats free of any clear diatonic or triadic progression. One analyst, Robert P. Morgan, has argued that it is the diminished seventh chord which includes B flat (B flat, D flat, E natural, G natural) rather than the tonic triad of B flat minor which possesses the determining structural function here, and that motion around this chord defines 'the final background structure of the Prelude'.[7] Morgan's interpretation is a further extension of Schenkerian analytical concepts into music which Schenker himself rejected out of hand. Indeed, the object of Morgan's analysis is to define 'a new kind of tonality' in which a more static, circular harmonic motion replaces the traditional background of functional tonality. Certainly the programmatic intent of this introduction, depicting Parsifal's weary wandering, may make the absence of a secure, concordant goal of any kind particularly appropriate, but it is only an introduction, and its procedures are replaced in the main body of the act by a more traditional emphasis on triadic harmony and third-related tonal centres. Coherence in the introduction is reinforced through repetition, sequence, the continued treatment of motivic elements, most of them already familiar. And with the entrance of Gurnemanz the music becomes more triadically focused: various orientations occur during the Gurnemanz–Kundry scene, including A flat/E flat at 'Der Winter floh und Lenz ist da!'; and a definite but incidental perfect cadence in D minor for Kundry's 'Dienen, dienen' confirms the D orientation hinted at at the very start of the scene, just before Gurnemanz's 'Von dorther kam das Stöhnen'.

During the passage immediately before Parsifal's entrance the prevailing chromaticism softens still further, and two interrupted cadences (in D minor and C minor) prepare the brief re-establishment of the A flat chord at 'Todesschlaf verscheuchen' before the harmony darkens again onto the diminished seventh (now with G as bass note) which ended the orchestral introduction. The simple gravity of the music as Parsifal appears is reinforced by the sombre orchestration. As Cosima reported, Wagner said: 'For Parsifal's entry I have horns *and* trumpets; horns alone seemed to me too soft, not ceremonial enough; trumpets alone too tinny, too clattery' (Diary, 18 December 1881).

Although the incidence of conventionally cadencing phrases increases during the first stage of the long scene between Gurnemanz and Parsifal, the cadences remain incidental, punctuating the flow rather than acting as points of focus for large areas of diatonic progression or extended tonal motion. An example of Wagner's technique at its most refined, as well as of his inspiration at its most profound, is provided by the long string melody to which Parsifal lays down his weapons, removes his helmet, and then prays before the spear. The melody has no obvious connection with any of the prevailing motives, but it provides perhaps the most poignant and eloquent line in the entire work: for Wagner himself it was the 'crux': 'it would be impossible to express what was happening at that moment with words' (see ex. 8).

ex. 8

But words can at least confirm that the intensity is such that tonality is in a state of suspension. The melody does eventually resolve by means of a perfect cadence in C sharp minor; but then there is a rapid shift onto a triad of G major — at Gurnemanz's 'Erkennst du ihn?' — announcing for the first time in Act III a tonal area which will achieve great importance later. As the scene proceeds, other cadential emphases occur to point up particularly decisive stages in the drama, such as the G flat cadence at the end of Parsifal's account of his wanderings — 'des

Grales heil'gen Speer' — which provides a much more positive conclusion to the developed material from the introduction than that heard
on its first appearance. This G flat resolution is briefly reinforced a little
later at Gurnemanz's 'Hier bist du; dies des Grals Gebiet'. Now it is
Gurnemanz's turn to describe what has happened at Monsalvat since
the end of Act I, and more explicit recapitulation of material from the
Act III introduction ensures a concentration of motivic process as well
as a continued avoidance of diatonic clarity: cadences are present, but
they tend to evade the full triadic presentation of one or both of the
chords concerned. The last of these cadences, when Gurnemanz describes the death of Titurel, provides the only strong confirmation of
the B flat minor orientation of so much of the music up to this point,
and it is immediately abandoned as Parsifal bursts in with 'Und ich,
ich bin's, der all' dies Elend schuf!'. The renewed chromaticism of his
renewed anguish strongly contrasts with Gurnemanz's calmer tonal
expansions: and with 'Die heil'ge Quelle selbst erquicke uns'res Pilgers
Bad' a rather tentative G major is established which will be strengthened
on repetition of this material at 'Gesegnet sei, du Reiner'. Nevertheless,
all that has happened so far is an increased degree of orientation around
G: the cadences are repeated, but there has been no large area of music
in either a pure or an expanded G major. Both E and B flat remain
alternative presences, as the interaction between 'Mir ahnt, ein hohes
Werk' and 'Gewisslich, uns'rer harrt die hehre Burg' indicates.

Gurnemanz's phrase 'Gesegnet sei. . .' presents another possible
derivative of example 1, and the dotted rhythm of its apex provides a
subtle link with the main melody of the Good Friday music (see ex. 9).

ex. 9

Gurnemanz

Ge - seg - - - net sei

Sehr zart und ausdrucksvoll

oboe p

One brief but strongly confirmed diatonic area precedes the Good Friday episode, the B major in which Gurnemanz anoints Parsifal. This paragraph contains relatively little chromatic expansion of its diatonic basis, appropriately determined by the two Parsifal themes dissolving into the Grail motive at 'entnimm nun seinem Haupt!', but the music grows much less stable immediately after the blessing itself, and although a pure B major re-emerges for the start of the Good Friday episode it does so through an interrupted cadence in E flat (D sharp) minor.

The principal tonal shift in the Good Friday scene itself is, again, through a third, from B to D major, with an initial cadential resolution at 'will ihr Gebet ihm weihen', and stronger confirmation after 'was all' da blüht und bald erstirbt'. The extremely rapid dissolution of the harmony after the final assertion of D at Parsifal's 'es lacht die Aue!' is a particularly impressive example of the extreme suppleness of the late Wagner style. It is, of course, a style in which heightened rhetoric results from extreme economy of utterance, and when the pervasively syllabic character of Parsifal's vocal line is diffused by the brief melisma at 'Segenstaue' the effect is almost that of a complete cadenza.

Much could be written on how the gentleness of the Good Friday music enshrines a pastoral spirituality totally absent from the Flower Maidens' seductive idyll: nature is not merely transformed from winter to spring, but from something dangerously artificial into something inspiringly real. And, with natural reality, comes once more the sense of space. Distant Monsalvat gradually impinges on the blissful forest scene, and the curiously archaic way in which the E minor orientation is introduced at 'Mittag, die Stund' ist da' adds further to the solemnity of the moment. This E accommodates the bells less comfortably than the C in the later stages of Act I, and the consequent tension is very evident in the transformation music, which resolves only at its very end into the B flat minor which, with B, D and G, have provided the principal points of tonal focus for the act so far.

The choral procession stays fairly close to this B flat minor centre, until the extraordinary tension induced by the incursion of the bells wrenches the tonal tendencies briefly across the tritone to E minor, though without clear cadential confirmation. Amfortas begins in a state of extreme agitation, but his salutation of Titurel provides cadential clarification of D minor, and this tonality is reinforced at 'dir gab ich den Tod'. The thematic material here is mainly concerned with Titurel, but Amfortas's very first words are accompanied by the opening theme of the Act III introduction on the violins – Parsifal's weary wandering is associated with Amfortas's death-desiring exhaustion.

After the D minor emphasis at 'dir gab ich den Tod' there are contrasting motions to D flat and A flat — complete with the Prelude's first theme — but then D reappears, changed from minor to major, at 'Dich ruf' ich', starting a phrase which then dissolves towards the disturbed E minor of the choral outbursts. Amfortas is driven to a final explosion of despair, and his own motive, peremptorily reiterated, breaks down before the surging tremolando of the forces of evil which, for him, are still potent. But, in a transition so swift as to be virtually impossible to realize effectively on the stage, Parsifal appears as the Grail theme overlays Amfortas's final agitated cry, and the brief stability of A major is reached at 'Nur eine Waffe taugt'. Melodically, this phrase is the merest counterpoint to the Grail theme in the orchestra and the rest of Parsifal's final address weaves in and out of the thematic complex spun so richly by the instruments. Such richness is indeed memorable, and moving, but what adds greatness to this peroration is the inexorably directed harmony. The initial A major is a close relative of both D and E, but it is not itself cadentially established, and functions rather as a larger-scale dominant to the emphatic resolution onto D major after 'dem zagen Toren gab'. Yet this itself, however appropriate symbolically as the key of Klingsor's defeat and the 'resolution' of Good Friday, is now only the chordal starting point for a progression through the distance of a tritone between D and the final tonal area of the work, A flat major, which is cadentially established as Parsifal completes his final phrase, 'Öffnet den Schrein!'. Everyone who experiences that extraordinarily potent shift of the harmony on the word 'Gral' in the final phrase must sense that the resolution it prepares is conclusive (see ex. 10).

ex. 10

Thus the entire choral and orchestral epilogue, with its synthesis of themes from the Act I Prelude embracing one passing reference to the Prophecy motive, provides a huge final expansion within the tonic chord of A flat. Secondary dominants are avoided, largely because of the determining presence of the Grail theme itself. The final stages of mediation and synthesis in the thematic process take place against a background of subtle tonal expansion, with prevailingly consonant harmony and lucidly opulent orchestration in which even the angelically pulsating harps do not seem too much of a good thing. But the tonal process itself is complete with Parsifal's own final note. What he celebrates in the epilogue is the more imposing for its certainty and stability.

V

This commentary on the music of *Parsifal* has concentrated on the identification and interpretation of harmonic and tonal features, not from any belief that the composer in some fundamental sense consciously organized his music around significant occurrences of particular progressions or degrees of tonal definition, but because the end result of his composing process was a tonal work of art. The musical themes, like the dramatic subject and text, clearly came first, but presenting and developing them was, for Wagner, a harmonic and tonal enterprise.

Such a brief commentary falls far short of analytical exhaustiveness: it merely introduces the issues and offers some suitable evidence. Given the huge amounts of published writing on Wagner, it may seem implausible to claim that an adequate musicological and analytical study of any of his music dramas has yet to appear. But biography and background have been far better served than technical commentary. Wagner's sketches have only recently become the object of extended and authoritative study, and the thorny issue of how he actually composed — strictly chronologically, transitions and all? — remains to be fully explored. From the analytical standpoint, moreover, there has been little serious discussion about what the most appropriate method might be, and even less agreement than discussion. I have mentioned three short commentaries on relatively brief extracts from *Parsifal*, but the best-known attempt at a comprehensive interpretation is one of the earliest, the fourth volume of Alfred Lorenz's *Das Geheimnis der Form bei Richard Wagner* (Berlin, 1933). This is not the place for either an exposition or a critique of Lorenz, but it is generally held today that he became the prisoner of his own belief that such evidently great works must be systematically as well as satisfyingly constructed.[8] While it might one day be possible to demonstrate in adequate detail that everything in a Wagner music drama relates in some valid sense to everything else, the subject-matter and characters being presented through an appropriately constructed text which then evokes motives, themes and textures, with their diatonic, expanded or floating tonal character, such a demonstration will surely confirm the supreme flexibility of the composer rather than his consistent application of predetermined principles of formal organization, whether 'secret' or not.

What cannot be denied is that worthwhile comparisons of style and technique between the dramas will only be possible when each has been adequately studied on its own. And the importance of an adequate basis for comparison is particularly acute in the case of *Parsifal*, since its very considerable differences from the earlier works can rebound to its disadvantage in summary accounts. The sufferings of Amfortas can seem pale beside those of Tristan, the machinations of Klingsor trivial beside those of Alberich and Hagen, the relationship of Kundry and Parsifal shallow beside that of Brünnhilde and Siegfried or Tristan and Isolde, the humanity and dignity of Gurnemanz limited beside that of Hans Sachs. As an assertion of personal charisma and an expression of collective beliefs, Parsifal's final oration can seem a good deal less compelling than its closer — if not very close — parallel, Sachs's address at the end of *Die Meistersinger*. But the validity of such comparisons depends on how far one is prepared to argue for an identity between 'pure' music drama and the *Bühnenweihfestspiel*. The music of *Parsifal* reflects the greater concern with those more passive yet responsive states of mind that rituals encourage; and Boulez can call it 'Wagner's most highly personal invention' because the dramatic theme of renunciation produces music in which the potential of the thematic material, whether chromatic or diatonic, is contemplated and explored with the greatest intensity, even if the music itself is often more reticent, more concentrated than is typical of the earlier works. In its contemplativeness and dismissal of the joys of the flesh, *Parsifal* complements the epic actions of the *Ring*, the sublime sensuality of *Tristan und Isolde*, the secular social preoccupations of *Die Meistersinger*. And its music has most to offer to those who fully appreciate the structural strength as well as the expressive power of the 'pure' music dramas which precede it and prepare for it.

Of course, *Parsifal* has not been universally admired, even when performed at Bayreuth: in 1912 Stravinsky 'sat humble and motionless, but after a quarter of an hour I could bear no more'.[9] Its immediate influence may indeed have been all to the bad, in that those composers who tried most sincerely to imitate it produced the least memorable music; but those most antipathetic to its manner might nevertheless find themselves drawn to its methods and subject-matter.[10] There was never the least point in attempting to imitate a composer of Wagner's stature, except as an academic exercise, and learning from him has been a protracted and traumatic affair. The story of that education is the history of twentieth-century music, in which Wagner has been cast as both Parsifal and Klingsor, saviour and devil: either he freed the language of music from its dependence on the exhausted hierarchies and formal stereotypes of tonally unified structures — pre-eminently the symphony — or he was primarily responsible, through destroying those structures, for the anarchy and self-indulgence which, in the view of its detractors, characterize much if not all modern music. Wagner is still the subject of polemics, and perhaps he himself would not have wished it otherwise. But the most fundamental lesson to be learned from all the music dramas, though most specifically from *Parsifal,* may well be that described by Boulez in the epigraphy to this chapter. Wagner may now be seen as the prophet of indeterminacy, of musical relativity, just as he has long been seen as the prophet of atonality. Most essentially of all, however, he was not a prophet, but a great composer in his own right. He may have been sincere when he said to Cosima in 1869 that 'in me the accent lies on the conjunction of poet and musician: as a pure musician I would not be of much significance' (Diary, 16 August 1869). Yet even though he put 'pure music' at the service of music drama, he is not merely supreme in the small company of great music dramatists, but pre-eminent among composers — even those for whom the theatre was the merest diversion. The hallmark of a great composer is not just the ability to invent memorable material, but the resourceful manipulation of that material to build satisfying, coherent structures. Wagner's unprecedented and unsurpassed innovations as a form-builder are, ultimately, the core of his greatness and the basis of his most profound and continuing influence.

4 *Stage history*

Many things which are accepted by the inner eye will hardly be tolerable during a performance. . .Ah, but the situations and their sequence — is that not the highest poetry?

> Nietzsche on the text of *Parsifal;* letter to Seydlitz 4 January 1878, quoted in J. P. Stern, *A study of Nietzsche,* p. 12

The stage history of *Parsifal* is unique: the presentation of no other dramatic work has been so intimately connected with a single theatre. In the first production, at the Bayreuth Festspielhaus in 1882, Wagner for the first time — *Rheingold* and *Die Walküre* had been produced in Munich before the 1876 Bayreuth *Ring* — presented to the world a new work directed by himself in his own theatre. *Parsifal* had been composed after the opening of the Festspielhaus, with performance in its particular acoustic and conditions in Wagner's mind. He called it *Ein Bühnen-weihfestspiel,* a Stage Dedication Festival Play, to distinguish it from the operas and music-dramas he had already written, and to confirm its connection with his festival theatre. In the century of its stage history that connection has altered and loosened, but has not been broken. For the first third of this hundred years, 1882-1914, performance of *Parsifal,* with a very few dissident exceptions, was confined to Bayreuth; for the second third, 1914 to World War II, performances throughout the operatic world closely conformed to the Bayreuth pattern set by Wagner and maintained by his widow and son; for the last third, 1951 to the present day, the model production of *Parsifal,* again with a few dissident exceptions, has been the new conception of the work presented in the post-war Bayreuth by Wieland Wagner, the composer's grandson. This summary is of course an over-simplification, but not, as we shall see, very much of one.

The 1882 *Parsifal* festival at Bayreuth, in which sixteen performances of the work were given in July and August, was universally reckoned to be a triumphant artistic success, however mixed were the judgements of

87

4 Wieland Wagner's set for the Good Friday meadow, Act III
Scene 1; Bayreuth 1956—62

the work itself. Wagner in the last summer of his life, and at the peak of his fame and prestige, was at last able to command resources of the variety and quality he had always sought. An orchestra of 107 players; a chorus of 135; 23 solo singers (including the six solo Flower Maidens, and alternative castings for Parsifal, Kundry, Gurnemanz and Klingsor) hand-picked from the opera houses of Germany; two conductors with nine musical assistants; and an outstandingly competent technical staff: all these people were assembled in Bayreuth, already note-perfect, three and a half weeks before the first performance, with their skill and experience entirely devoted to a single object. The achievement of such conditions for the performance of opera, even more than the building of his own theatre, was the fulfilment of an ambition Wagner had nursed ever since the frustrations of his youth in the German theatre of the 1830s and 1840s. A run of sixteen performances, for example, uninterrupted by repertory intrusions, was an unheard-of privilege for an operatic production: Wagner himself, in his retrospective essay 'Das Bühnenweihfestspiel in Bayreuth' written in Venice in November 1882, said that the enthusiasm of the cast and orchestra and the beauty of their presentation steadily increased as the performances went on.

The essay gives a clear impression of the constructive and co-operative atmosphere of the festival, of the composer at his best, flexible and practical among the complexities of operatic production, and of the dedication of the many people involved. He was asked, Wagner says,

what principle of authority, organized to the last detail and yet capable of responding to the smallest requirement, guided the astonishingly precise execution of this scenic, musical and dramatic event, on, under, behind and in front of the stage; I replied cheerfully that anarchy had done it, according to which everyone had done what he *wanted*, that is to say, what he had to do.[1]

This is naturally a rosy view of obediently accepted autocracy; 'everybody wanted the same as I wanted', Wagner had said in a letter to Ludwig in September. Nevertheless it remains true that harmony, disturbed by only a minimum of jealousy among the leading singers, prevailed at the festival and that a very high standard of performance was obtained. Wagner demanded clarity and intelligibility above all from his singers — it is here that he makes his famous recommendation to prefer the little notes to the big ones — and banished such operatic habits as extravagant gesture and the turning to the audience for effect. He praises the Flower Maidens in particular for their understanding that they should sing in a naive, childlike manner, without seductive passion;

and insists on the necessity for an austere presentation of the Grail temple scenes. The knights should be monastic in their demeanour and Amfortas not distinguished in appearance from the rest.

Detailed production notes survive, and are printed in *Richard Wagner: Sämtliche Werke* (vol. xxx, 1970). Those taken by Anton Schittenhelm, a singer from the Vienna Opera, for his colleague Theodor Reichmann the first Amfortas, contain sketches of stage positions – thirteen for the first act alone – which give a precise idea of Wagner's direction of his cast. Other observations by various participants and witnesses record exact movements, delivery of words, pauses, small changes in the text, instructions for the orchestra and stage-hands, all preserved by Cosima after Wagner's death as a guarantee of fidelity to the Master's intentions in future productions. Wagner had said (to Cosima in 1878): 'How I detest all the business of costumes and make-up. . . , after creating the invisible orchestra, I should like to invent the invisible theatre as well.'[2] He threw himself nevertheless, sparing neither himself nor anyone else into the precise realization of this drama conceived almost forty years before: he knew what he wanted and it is clear from his essay that, with one or two exceptions, he got it. This was a model production in every sense. What was it like?

The orchestral playing, singing and acting in those first performances were probably as good as, and in some cases better than, any since. Wagner himself warmly praised the conductor, Hermann Levi, and the orchestra, who were mainly drawn from the Munich Court company. Some of the most successful singers had previous experience of the house and of Wagner's exigent demands as a producer: Amalie Materna and Marianne Brandt, who alternated with Therese Malten as Kundry, had sung Brünnhilde and Waltraute respectively at Bayreuth in 1876. Karl Hill's Klingsor was reckoned at least as striking and sinister as his 1876 Alberich. Most admired of all, however, was the Gurnemanz of Emil Scaria, a singer new to Bayreuth, who was to become the best Wotan of the day.

The visual aspect of the production is, of course, the only one about which certainty is now possible. The sets and costumes were designed by Paul von Joukowsky, a young Russian painter who had been more or less living with the Wagners for several years and was therefore in close contact with the creation of the work. His greatest triumph was the design for the Grail temple, inspired by the interior of Siena Cathedral where Wagner in the summer of 1880 had been moved to tears by the beauty of the building. This set, with its dome rising out of sight, its stepped plinth for the altar of the Grail in the centre of circular sanctuary, and its columned side-aisles receding into darkness, was perfectly suited to the requirements of the work, particularly to the converging approach of the two processions in the third act. The sets for Act I Scene 1 and for the Good Friday meadow were unexceptionably naturalistic in the style of the time. Act II, with its two rapid and visible transformations, from Klingsor's tower to magic garden and from magic garden to desert, was managed with a technical skill which much impressed contemporaries, the actual sets following to the letter the instructions in the score, and the magic garden deriving from the Palazzo Rufolo garden in Ravello which Wagner and Joukowsky had visited together. The long transformations in the first and third acts had a series of continuous backcloths designed for them which were to unroll behind the slowly pacing figures of Parsifal and Gurnemanz to give the impression of their mysterious journeys from the forest into the secret interior of the Grail temple. This device caused a good deal of trouble: in the end, to Wagner's disgust, the music for the Act I transformation had to be repeated, with the addition of a few bars by Humperdinck (one of the musical assistants), while the scenery for the Act III transformation was abandoned and the music performed to a dropped curtain.

Joukowsky's costumes were mostly inoffensive belted robes, much simpler and more generally acceptable than the *Ring* costumes of 1876 had been. Costumes for the Flower Maidens, however, presented him with problems which he solved to Wagner's but not to universal satisfaction. Felix Weingartner's conclusion on them, 'Their costumes are tasteless, quite incomprehensibly tasteless, but their singing is beyond all praise',[3] was widely shared. Maurice Kufferath, a sympathetic and perceptive critic of the work as a whole, thought the magic garden scene crude and ugly. Kundry reclined among garish flowers, dressed in a courtesan's ball-gown with draped garlands and strings of pearls. 'She really ought to lie like a Titian Venus, in naked beauty', Wagner had said, wistfully and impractically, when he saw Joukowsky's costume design.

Wagner died six months after his *Parsifal* festival. In the two following summers (1883 and 1884) the production was revived at Bayreuth with Levi again conducting and under the artistic direction first of Scaria and then of Anton Fuchs, who had alternated with Hill as Klingsor in 1882. There was no festival in 1885, and only in 1886, when her new production of *Tristan* was performed with *Parsifal*, did Cosima Wagner assume overt control of the theatre. A full and most impressive account, by Charles and Pierre Bonnier, of the *Parsifal* production in these early years appeared in the *Revue wagnérienne* of April 1887. It is clear from this essay that the essential contrasts between scenes and acts dictated by the score were successfully achieved. The second act, in which zig-zag lines, bizarre shapes and obscure shadows filled the stage, was set against the serene lighting and ordered movements of the first and third acts, in which 'vertical and horizontal lines balance each other'. This contrast, of course, reflected the contrast between the diatonic music of the Grail and Parsifal, and the chromatic anguish of Klingsor and Kundry, a point reinforced by the Bonniers when they remark upon the monstrous luxuriance of flowers and vegetation in the magic garden, against which was placed 'the simple, calm silhouette of Parsifal'. A further effective contrast they describe is that between the bland and unmysterious woodland atmosphere of Act I Scene 1 and the 'great void that occupies the stage' as Gurnemanz and Parsifal arrive in the temple of the Grail, 'at the same time as the acoustic undergoes a definite change on account of the deep space'. Most striking of all is the difference they noticed between the two scenes in the Grail temple. In the first, the Grail ceremony had a remote, dream-like quality, while Parsifal, observing it, seemed to disappear from the spectator's consciousness and then reappear as the vision of the Grail and its entourage vanished leaving the boy and Gurnemanz alone in the empty hall. In the second, the action, in which Parsifal is a participant, took place at the front of the stage and had a contrasting powerful reality, 'dramatic and violent'. It is also plain from this essay that Wagner's direction of the characters of Parsifal and particularly Kundry (who has to act much more of the time than she has to sing) was subtle, clear and effective through the whole length of the work.

Carl Dahlhaus has pointed out that 'Bayreuth was the institutionalization in musical practice of a principle that the musical scholarship of the same period was documenting in the first historico-critical editions',[4] the principle, that is, of the authentic version. This was so true of *Parsifal* that Wagner refused to allow the possibility of its performance in any other theatre: if the public wished to see this last and loftiest work, then the public must take the trouble to come to Bayreuth, where yearly performances for all time were proposed, to see it correctly presented. In July 1881 he expressed doubts to his banker Feustel about the propriety of publishing even a piano arrangement of the score for these reasons. The only serious attempt to persuade him to relent was made by Angelo Neumann, the impresario who devoted years of successful effort to the touring of the *Ring* and other Wagner operas throughout Europe. In October 1881 Neumann managed to elicit from

Wagner a vague promise that, despite his wish that *Parsifal* should be performed only in Bayreuth, he might one day entrust the work to a travelling Wagner theatre. During the 1882 festival, however, when Neumann presented him with a contract handing over exclusive rights for the production of *Parsifal* outside Bayreuth, Wagner, 'with his pen poised over the paper', asked 'as a great favour' to be released from his promise. Neumann agreed.[5] This episode effectively confined the production of the work to Bayreuth for the next thirty years. In a letter to Neumann in September 1882, confirming his decision, Wagner gave as his reason 'the lofty character of the work itself'. Although he goes on to suggest that, should his own powers fail before his death, he might concede to Neumann personally the right to put on 'certain festival performances at stated occasions', one sentence reveals a more practical motive for his present refusal: 'My creation of *Parsifal* shall stand or fall with Bayreuth.'[6] The drawing power of a work which could not be seen elsewhere was not lost on Wagner, as Houston Stewart Chamberlain confirms in his *Richard Wagner*. Wagner, he says, at first contemplated the performance of all his earlier works at Bayreuth. 'Afterwards, when the project had been abandoned, and the continuation of the festival plays was dependent more particularly on the power of *Parsifal* to attract an audience, Wagner announced his intention of giving one of his older works every year, together with *Parsifal.*'[7] With the exception of 1896, when the *Ring* was revived for the first time, this pattern – *Parsifal,* with one, two or three other Wagner works – was established by Cosima at each of her festivals, and maintained under the direction of Siegfried Wagner (1908–30) and his widow Winifred (1931–44). The festivals, however, were not held annually until 1936, and from 1940 to 1944 *Parsifal,* for reasons which are not entirely clear, was not performed.

Cosima Wagner took over the direction of Bayreuth (a development which had never occurred to Wagner himself) because she realized that the production of *Parsifal* was slipping back from Wagner's high standards. Her object was to see that her husband's intentions should continue, as far as possible, to be carried out: the strict confinement of *Parsifal* to the festival theatre was one of them. The ban on other productions was maintained by Cosima's will-power and eventually effected through the newly regularized copyright laws. The Berne Convention, binding most European countries to mutual copyright agreement, was signed in 1887. The copyright period was set at thirty years after the death of the author. European Wagner enthusiasts who could not see *Parsifal* at Bayreuth had to make do with concert performances and orchestral extracts. Only in Amsterdam did Cosima allow, in 1905, a private staged performance mounted by the city's Wagner Society. America, on the other hand, was party to no international copyright agreement until 1909. A production at the Metropolitan in New York, in 1903, was put on with a lavish expenditure of time, money and care which made it, in the words of the *New York Times* (26 December 1903), 'without doubt the most perfect production ever made on the American lyric stage'. The sets and machinery, which functioned flawlessly, were supervised by Anton Fuchs and reproduced as exactly as possible those at Bayreuth; the singers of Parsifal, Kundry, Gurnemanz and Amfortas had all been coached at Bayreuth by Cosima. They were punished for their treachery by not being invited to sing again in the festival theatre. This production was a huge success: New York must have been at the time in the grip of rampant Wagner mania since the whole *Ring, Tannhäuser, Lohengrin* and *Tristan* were all also given at the Metropolitan in that same season. An English version of *Parsifal* opened in Boston in October 1904 and toured several other American and Canadian cities.

Otherwise Bayreuth retained its hold on *Parsifal* until 1913, with the exception of the almost incredible number of eight private performances given by Bayreuth casts for Ludwig, entirely alone in the Munich Court Opera, in 1884 and 1885. In 1913 there were a charity production in Monte Carlo (in French; one of the triumphs of the remarkable director, Raoul Gunsbourg), a public production in Zurich (the Swiss copyright had expired), and, astonishingly, Italian performances in Buenos Aires and in Rio de Janeiro. With the expiry of the Berne Convention copyright at midnight on 31 December 1913, the opera houses of Europe, many of whom had sanctimoniously condemned the Metropolitan in 1903, burst into productions of *Parsifal* with a unanimity which shows to what an extraordinary pitch enthusiasm for Wagner had climbed in the years immediately before the First World War. There were productions of *Parsifal* in more than fifty European cities between 1 January and 1 August 1914. It was performed at all the major opera houses (Milan, Vienna, Paris, Berlin, London, Rome, Venice, St Petersburg), in German, Italian, French, Russian, Czech and Flemish. (By 1938 *Parsifal* had also been performed in Danish, Swedish, Dutch Croatian, Hungarian, Romanian, Finnish, Slovenian, Lettish and Serbian.) If Wagner had intended to whet the appetite of the opera-going world for *Parsifal* by ensuring its confinement to Bayreuth for so long, he certainly succeeded.

These productions stayed as close to the Bayreuth model as the managements of the opera houses could afford. The largest houses hired singers trained in their roles at Bayreuth and copied the production with any first-hand assistance available. At La Scala (Milan), where the first performance, in Italian, on 9 January 1914, was conducted by Serafin, the sets and machinery, as in New York, were supervised by Fuchs, now sixty-five years old and clearly reckoned to be the leading authority on *Parsifal* transformations. In Paris (4 January 1914), to which special trains ran from London, the Parsifal was Cosima's best exponent of the role, Ernest van Dyck, singing the part for the first time in French. In Vienna (25 January 1914), where vast amounts of money were spent on extremely elaborate and accident-prone scenery, twenty-seven performances were given in the first year, of a production whose opening cast included a Parsifal, a Gurnemanz and a Kundry (Schmedes, Mayr and the great Anna Bahr-Mildenburg) with Bayreuth experience of the roles.

London audiences had heard excerpts from *Parsifal* since as early as October 1882 when the Prelude was performed in a Saturday Concert at the Crystal Palace. In 1913 Sir Henry Wood had arranged and conducted an abbreviated version of the score, without voices, at the Coliseum, to accompany a series of 'living tableaux' designed by Byam Shaw. The recently built Coliseum, the largest theatre in London, was a music-hall at the time; as Richard Northcott patronizingly wrote in 1914, 'the opera was thus brought to the notice of thousands who would never enter Covent Garden or a concert hall'.[8] The first full production, however, opened at Covent Garden on 2 February 1914. Trouble and expense in the cause of fidelity to Bayreuth, here as elsewhere, were not spared. Grail bells were specially cast; props, including the Grail itself, that had been used for Ludwig's personal performances were borrowed from Munich; Willi Wirk, a Bayreuth technical assistant, was the stage-manager. Several of the leading singers, including Hensel and Vogl (Parsifal), Knüpfer (Gurnemanz), and Bender (Amfortas), had sung at Bayreuth. The twelve planned performances were sold out and two more added; every seat under £1 for the whole season was sold before the opening, some, perhaps, to Northcott's 'thousands'. This would have pleased Wagner; the actual performances might have pleased him less. Adrian Boult, who toured the provinces conducting an English *Parsifal* in 1926, was a musical assistant at Covent Garden in 1914 and remembers Artur Bodansky's conducting as 'noisy and unsympathetic'; the chorus of knights was so weak that they had to be augmented by half the violas from the orchestra, the players hiding behind the cardboard pillars of the Grail temple.

Before the expiry of the copyright, Cosma Wagner had mounted a campaign to persuade the Reichstag in Berlin to pass a special 'Lex Parsifal', confining the performance of the work to Bayreuth for ever. Although the campaign failed, the subservience to Bayreuth evident in the 1914 productions showed a universal desire not to deviate from the master's 'authentic version' that must have been some consolation to her. It did not falter for many years: the original Covent Garden production was not superseded until 1959 and was last seen in 1951; at the Metropolitan some of the 1903 sets were still in use in 1955.

Meanwhile at Bayreuth itself Siegfried Wagner had taken over the administration of the festival theatre from his mother in 1908; after his death in 1930 he was succeeded by his widow, Winifred. The composer's original *Parsifal* production was the mainstay of the festival throughout these years; nor did the flood of productions elsewhere deflect the attendance of audiences at Bayreuth. Singers, of course, came and went; after Cosima's retirement they were more flexibly directed and more allowance was made for individual variations of talent and interpretation. But the style of the production was guaranteed by the use of most of the 1882 sets and by a remarkable continuity in the conducting succession. Levi conducted *Parsifal* at Bayreuth from 1882 until 1894. After 1897, when Mottl and Seidl both conducted it, Fischer, Levi's assistant in 1882, undertook it for the 1899 festival. From 1901 until 1930 Karl Muck conducted the work at every festival, sometimes sharing it with Balling, Kaehler, and, in 1909 only, with Siegfried Wagner. For half a century, therefore, *Parsifal* at Bayreuth was in the hands of conductors of the central Wagner tradition; both Balling and Kaehler had worked at Bayreuth since 1896.

Only the sets for Act II, always the least satisfactory of the original production, were changed during this period. Siegfried began to tinker with the magic garden in 1912. Because of the Great War and financial difficulties created for Bayreuth by the ending of all the other, lucrative, Wagner copyrights in 1913, there was no festival between 1914 and 1924. When Siegfried reopened the theatre he employed a new designer, Kurt Söhnlein, to help him modernize some of the existing festival productions, in particular to change the flat scenery of the past into three-dimensional sets. Söhnlein inserted a new Klingsor's tower, vaguely Indian in style, into the 1925 *Parsifal,* and in 1927 the whole of Act II was redesigned, with white gauzes and transparent flowers in changing light for the magic garden and a third, more abstract, Klingsor's tower. The model of the magic garden set which survives at Bayreuth suggests that this was one of the more successful attempts to solve the problems of Act II. The rebuilding of the two front columns of the Grail temple in solid form was Söhnlein's only other modification of Joukowsky's sets.

Siegfried and Cosima Wagner died in 1930. Under Winifred Wagner's regime at Bayreuth, several changes overtook *Parsifal*. Between 1931 and 1939, Toscanini, Strauss, Furtwängler and von Hoesslin conducted the work, Toscanini considerably more slowly than anyone else before or since. In 1934 Alfred Roller, the great Wagner designer—director who had worked with Mahler in Vienna, was hired to replace Joukowsky's sets and costumes with a completely new *Parsifal*. No pictorial record survives of this production, which seems to have been generally disappointing. For its first revival in 1936, Heinz Tietjen, Winifred's festival director, entrusted the very young Wieland Wagner, Siegfried and Winifred's son, with the task of improving the sets: he designed a new Good Friday meadow. In the following year Wieland Wagner, still only twenty, persuaded Tietjen, with whom he was already on cool terms, to allow him to design new sets for the whole work. His painted designs, to which these sets were built, show modification of the Joukowsky tradition in the direction of simplicity but by no means a break with it. In the Grail temple, for example, Joukowsky's columned distances were closed off by a solid back wall, with doors at either side for the entry of the knights, but the basic shape of the set as a domed church interior with clusters of pillars and round arches remained. The old transformation device of scenery moved across rollers was, however, replaced by cinematic projections which could be controlled to match the conductor's tempo. Much of the public reaction to Wieland's designs was favourable, but the Bayreuth old guard, represented by his aunt Daniela and Karl Muck, were shocked by deviations, modest though they were, from the *Parsifal* to which they had been accustomed for more than fifty years.

Behind these somewhat half-hearted attempts to modify what remained, in effect, the whole operatic world's conception of Wagner's last work lay the, mostly unacknowledged, influence of Adolphe Appia. This Swiss designer and perceptive critic of Wagner's dramas had, almost alone, in 1882, as an acute twenty-year-old, been puzzled by the gulf he felt between the power of the score of *Parsifal* and what he saw as the weakness and conventional theatricality of its visual presentation. He went on to write two books, *La mise-en-scène du drame wagnérien* (1895) and *Die Musik und die Inszenierung* (1899), in which he insisted on the necessity for three-dimensional sets and for a new imaginative use of lighting as the most important element in production. He also, and more fundamentally, pointed to the need to ignore some of the composer's precise instructions, which had issued from the ponderous realism of the late nineteenth-century theatre. From this, according to Appia, Wagner had never detached himself, as he had from the rest of contemporary operatic convention, so that the visual embodiment of his productions had lagged behind, and remained at odds with, the inner vision expressed in the words and music. Although Cosima had condemned Appia's ideas as unnecessary in the face of Wagner's specific legacy of production requirements, Söhnlein's solid columns and reliance on changing light show the beginning of his influence at Bayreuth, while Roller had elsewhere produced several Wagner works in accordance with his ideas. As Hitler's demands assumed priority at Bayreuth, however, Tietjen and his designer Preetorius went in for increasingly lavish realistic productions of the other works, all the time moving further away from Appia's theories, and after 1939 *Parsifal*, as we have seen, was not performed in Winifred's Bayreuth.

When the theatre was reopened in 1951, under the direction of Wieland Wagner and his brother Wolfgang, a new *Parsifal*, a revolutionary production which was to last, in its turn, for a quarter of a century, astonished everyone who saw it. Wieland Wagner had spent the intervening years in intensive study of Wagner's scores, in some productions of his own outside Bayreuth, and in a period of bitter disillusionment, exile and poverty in which the post-war continuation of the festival must often have seemed a hopeless prospect. His 1951 *Parsifal*, the longest-lived and perhaps the most entirely successful of all his productions, was the fruit of these years. In it the influence of Appia's books was absorbed and transcended. Whereas Appia's designs for *Parsifal* — sketched in 1896 but never realized — had been of heavy three-dimensional sets, tree-trunks to double as columns for the first and third acts, and a powerful realistic keep for Klingsor, Wieland Wagner dispensed with almost all scenery. He used plain backdrops for the outdoor scenes, and his Grail temple was reduced to the bones of Joukowsky's design: four plain columns framing a circular area where the knights, in a solemn ring, surrounded Amfortas and the Grail, the whole scene dimly lit against a background of mysterious darkness. Lighting was the principal visual feature of the whole production, cool greys and blues conveying the early mornings of Act I Scene 1 and Act III Scene 1, and shifting violet the seductive menace of the magic garden. Klingsor compelling Kundry to his purpose was brightly lit and remote at the centre of a suggested tower or spider's web, surrounded by gloomy shadows. The action of the whole work took place on an illuminated disc in the centre of the stage.

The impact of the 1951 Bayreuth *Parsifal* was tremendous. Much disliked by some, as a denial of Wagner's scenic intentions, it struck others as a revelation of the work's substance. Ernest Newman, nearing the end of a long life devoted to Wagner, called it 'the best *Parsifal* I have ever seen', and explained: 'We were conscious, for the first time, of the characters as Wagner must have seen them in his creative imagination, and the music, with nothing intruding now between it and us, spoke to us with a poignancy beyond the power of words to express.' These phrases recall Wagner's paradoxical wish to 'invent an invisible theatre', and go some way towards indicating the magnitude of Wieland Wagner's achievement. Although he tended to deny all influences and, defending his *Parsifal* in 1951, attributed it to 'many years of work, the knowledge I have gained, and. . .all that I have so far experienced and suffered',[9] there is no doubt that, at the very least, he shared Appia's conception of the work. His designs may have looked quite different; his successful interiorization of the drama was exactly what Appia had prescribed so many years before. 'Strictly speaking,' Wieland Wagner wrote to the horrified Hans Knappertsbusch, who nevertheless (except in 1953) conducted the Bayreuth *Parsifal* every year from 1951 until 1964, 'the scenery in *Parsifal* is nothing but the expression of the changing moods of Parsifal's soul, whose "path to salvation". . .it is the director's job to reveal.'[10] Appia had written, more precisely, in 1897:

In *Parsifal*, the visual aspect consists of a series of diverse scenes which are there for the sole purpose of working a miraculous transformation in the hero's pure and unconscious soul; Parsifal through them becomes conscious of himself, and by means of his chastity is able at the same time to extend his knowledge to all living things: supreme unity is thus revealed to him.[11]

Wieland Wagner said of his 1951 Good Friday meadow:

The essential thing for my production was that this scene would represent the achievement. . .of ultimate spiritual clarity and an understanding of the ultimate conditions of the world, rather than a romantic experience of nature, which, of course, would be far better represented by means of a few birches and Gurnemanz's hut.[12]

Appia's set for Act III Scene 1 had included trees, rocks, a spring, and Gurnemanz's hut. Wieland Wagner's was an empty space and a lit circle, in which Parsifal, Gurnemanz and Kundry were grouped beside the planted spear: it fulfilled, as nearly as, perhaps, is possible, the requirements of Appia's subtlest passage on the work:

[Parsifal's] inner evolution, the drama's subject, is expressed entirely by the music. . .What is seen, on the other hand, and has to cause this evolution, is, in the absolute sense, undetermined: only suffering can evoke compassion, but there are a thousand kinds of suffering. In consequence, the 'story' in *Parsifal* assumes a peculiarly arbitrary quality. To avoid too great a strain between it and the elevated level of the musical content, the visible scenes must be placed in some kind of ideal realm where the meaning of the episodes can spontaneously become universal, and match the internal world which the music reveals.

Appia added, somewhat wrily: 'Nevertheless the problem of presentation is so far only defined, not solved.'[13] Many who saw Wieland Wagner's 1951 *Parsifal* thought that they had seen the problem solved.

Wieland Wagner himself, however, altered and adjusted his production almost continuously during the remaining fifteen years of his life. 'What is left of the 1951 production now?', he said in 1964. 'The disc, the temple of the Grail, the holy lake. Otherwise everything is different. . .Because we have been constantly working on it, nobody has noticed.'[14] The changes he made were mostly in the sets for the magic garden of Act II and the Good Friday meadow of Act III Scene 1: scenes closely related to each other by Parsifal's apprehension of the contrast between them and of Kundry's transformation within them. After 1955 the empty stage acquired an amorphous circular shape in the background of the magic garden, and contrasting straight verticals, suggesting tree-trunks, for the meadow. In 1963 these were replaced by wavy, fiery lines of vegetation in the garden and fine straight lines with thin arcs suggesting branches in the meadow: it is interesting that this contrast echoes exactly that noticed by the Bonniers in the original production, although the means used were so much reduced and refined.

When Knappertsbusch died after the 1965 performances, which had been conducted by the Belgian, André Cluytens, Wieland Wagner invited Pierre Boulez to take over the work. After so many years he wanted to stress a central fact which his production perfectly matched: 'Parsifal is Wagner's natural route from hyper-romanticism to clarity; to a clarity which closely approaches modern music in its structures.'[15] But in the summer of 1966 Wieland Wagner was himself very ill (he died on 17 October of that year), and had to direct the festival with notes written from hospital. 'It is very bitter for me,' he wrote to the chorus-master Wilhelm Pitz, 'that I cannot be present this year in particular, when I had set myself to bring out a completely new *Parsifal* in the staging, singing and in the chorus work.'[16] The Boulez–Wieland Wagner *Parsifal*, which its director never witnessed, was nevertheless widely considered to be one of the peaks of achievement in post-war Bayreuth.

In 1975 Wieland's brother Wolfgang replaced the 1951 *Parsifal* with a new production. The stage was bedecked with the leaves and flowers of a moderate realism; only the Grail temple retained an economy almost as stark as Wieland's. This production is a well-judged compromise, which makes less stringent demands upon director and cast than the 1951 production, but which also cannot attain the purity glimpsed by Appia and described by Wieland Wagner as 'mystical expression of a very complex state of the soul, rooted in the unreal and grasped only by intuition'.[17]

Outside Bayreuth there have been, of course, since the second World War, many new productions of *Parsifal*. But, just as for several decades Richard Wagner succeeded in imposing on the entire operatic world his own conception of the work, so Wieland Wagner's idea of *Parsifal* became the norm for a whole generation. The Metropolitan in 1956 and Covent Garden in 1959 are examples of major houses which mounted long-lived productions closely modelled on Bayreuth's although less drastic in the paring down of scenery and movement. Two productions at the San Carlo in Naples (1954 and 1967) were strikingly successful in assimilating the influence of Wieland Wagner while retaining a sense of sunlit Mediterranean space which would have delighted the composer. Filippo Sanjust at Berlin in 1975 filled an almost empty stage with complicated lighting, its colour and intensity frequently altering. Some Wieland-influenced productions, staged without his own fierce discipline, have perhaps lost as much as they have gained by his example. If every movement and every lighting-direction is not thought out with complete attention, it may be safer to stick to the trees and rocks of 1882.

Elsewhere a few opera houses, in conscious revolt against an orthodoxy which had quickly become, though not by Wieland's intention, as powerful as Wagner's own, attempted something altogether different. Frankfurt in 1959 staged a *Parsifal* in which heavy mosaic sets abolished the essential distinctions between the scenes. Kassel in 1970 adopted an ugly science-fiction surrealism which cleverly solved the transformation problems but destroyed the sense of the earth and its innocence without which the Good Friday climax means little. Götz Friedrich in Stuttgart in 1976 presented a neon-lit *Parsifal* in abstract sets which inflicted the same loss on the realm of the Grail while achieving a strong and frightening second act. Terry Hands at Covent Garden in 1979 showed only how vulnerable the work can be to a clutter of arbitrary objects, excessive lighting changes, and undisciplined and ceaseless movement.

Parsifal has now become part of the normal operatic repertory, as Wieland Wagner, unlike his grandfather, believed that it should (*'Parsifal* is better instrumented than any other Wagner work, and it is easier to find the players for it.').[18] The fact, indicated by its stage history, that productions depart from the Bayreuth model, whether old or new, at their peril, may seem nevertheless to suggest that Wagner was right to think his last work uniquely suited to his own theatre and to the atmosphere of devoted concentration which the Bayreuth festival engenders. The truth is perhaps less simple, although more practical. 'Richard Wagner worked on *Parsifal* for thirty years', said Wieland in 1964. 'There was no problem that he did not fully consider.'[19] The same was true of Wieland himself. In the year of his death, thirty years after his first design for the Good Friday meadow, he said:

What does depth-psychology aim at? To interpret, clarify, sift. The music in *Parsifal* has the same function. . .In *Parsifal* Wagner became an architect. The whole work is fundamentally derived from the first theme, and is very sharply structured. It is clear, well-constructed, cohesive music, the music of a composer who did not want to stop at the level of earlier achievements.[20]

The coherence and symmetry of the work must be embodied in production. The two Grail scenes must be related and differentiated in the ways indicated by the score; the two outdoor scenes in the realm of the Grail, and therefore the whole first act and the whole third act, must similarly be related and differentiated; the second act must be connected to them by the contrast between Titurel's kingdom and Klingsor's; in particular the magic garden — evil, enclosed and transient — of Klingsor's defeated power must be related to the flowery meadow of the rescued Grail — innocent, open and eternal. If all this has been better achieved at Bayreuth than elsewhere, it is because the director's understanding of the work has there been deeper. And if the achievement of 1951 in some ways surpassed that of 1882, it was because progress in theatrical technique had made it possible for the presentation of the work to match the conception Wagner himself had expressed only in his score. What Wagner failed to visualize and Appia had hoped for as a theoretical goal, Wieland Wagner, with his intellectual rigour and austere continence in the use of means, set forth in a production which is likely to remain the most satisfying that the work will ever receive.

5 Reactions and critical assessments

The Germans are really peculiar people! They make life more difficult
for themselves than is necessary by seeking everywhere, and putting
into everything, their profound thoughts and ideas. . .A poetic creation
is the better for being incommensurable and rationally incomprehensible.

Goethe to Eckermann 6 May 1827[1]

I

All kinds of distinguished people came to Bayreuth for the 1882
Parsifal. Composers, writers, painters and, of course, critics flocked to
admire, or merely to inspect, the new opera, the odd theatre and the
old man who together formed the most striking cultural phenomenon
of the age. Wagner's last work could not fail to produce a discordant
babel of conflicting comment. The neurotic peculiarity of its characters
and the apparently undramatic determinism of its plot were objected
to by many. The Christian elements in the work were considered
blasphemous by some, irrelevant by others, an easy route to superficial
comprehension by yet others, and a betrayal of the principles of truth
and freedom by Nietzsche. Opinions as to the quality of the music
similarly varied between widely distant extremes. Some spectators were
frankly bored: Delibes shocked d'Indy by saying that he liked the
second act because there were pretty girls. But Eduard Hanslick, of the
Vienna *Neue Freie Presse*, the most famous music critic of the day, was
also bored by long stretches of *Parsifal*, and also preferred the Flower
Maidens' chorus to any other part of the work.

Among the early reactions, awed admiration was less articulate than
disapproval. Liszt clearly spoke for many when he wrote to Wolzogen
after the first performance: 'During and after yesterday's performance
the general feeling was that there is nothing that can be said about this
miraculous work. Silence is surely the only possible response to so
deeply moving a work; the solemn beat of its pendulum is from the

103

5 Wieland Wagner's set for the Good Friday meadow, Act III
Scene 1; Bayreuth 1963—73

sublime to the most sublime.'[2] Nevertheless, attempts to dissect *Parsifal's* faults by those who did not like it, and attempts to account for its splendours by those who did, soon multiplied. No semblance of a critical consensus was arrived at in the first decade of prolific comment, nor has such a consensus been achieved in the subsequent ninety years. If one extreme view, that which saw *Parsifal* as a simple work of Christian edification, has faded, the other, seeing it as vicious in content and evil in influence, has recently strengthened. Between the two extremes is no centre point but an assortment of evaluations and analyses on different levels, arrived at from different preconceptions. This chapter will attempt, by means of an annotated anthology of critical writing, to give some idea of the variety of views that have been held, and of the nature of the judgements made by the most interesting minds that have applied themselves to the subject.

Hanslick's despatches from Bayreuth in 1882 provide a good starting-point, not only because of his deserved pre-eminence among the critics present, but because his well-argued suspicion of the whole Wagnerian enterprise and particularly of the dubious exaltations which he found in *Parsifal* are representative of a strong school of thought. That the musical tradition should become contaminated by specific content of such a questionable kind was, in Hanslick's view, a menace to be resisted. When Stravinsky in 1911, in full reaction against Wagner, walked out of *Parsifal*, his protest was essentially the same as Hanslick's, and the musical case against Wagner has not changed since Hanslick's original formulation of it. It underlies both his superficial and his profound misunderstandings of *Parsifal*.

Hanslick's first essay sets out his case against the text of the drama:

The listener who is sufficiently naive to conceive of the Wagnerian *Parsifal* as a kind of superior magic opera, as a free play of fantasy revelling in the wondrous, will catch the best aspect of it and salvage the least troubled pleasure. He will have to defend himself only against the false notion that beneath it all lies an unfathomably profound, holy meaning, a philosophic and religious revelation. Unfortunately, it is upon this alleged deep, moral significance, upon the Christian–mystical element in Wagner's poem, that the greatest weight is laid. And about this aspect of the new *Bühenweihfestspiel* and its dramatic physiognomy I have grave reservations.

Just as in most Wagnerian works the dramatic kernel, clothed in brilliant raiment, is sickly and meagre because the characters behave less according to their own free will than according to the will of supernatural powers, so it is in *Parsifal,* and even more so than in any of Wagner's earlier works. In everyone involved there is wanting precisely that which makes for dramatic character: free self-determination in good or bad. . .

The Holy Grail is all, signifies all, and decides all. What is the Grail to us? A legendary curiosity, a long-forgotten superstition, foreign both to popular and enlightened consciousness. The hysterical exaltation incessantly associated with the Holy Grail, the Holy Lance, and the Holy Blood in Wagner's *Parsifal* finds no response today in German minds and German hearts, and never will. . .

We can almost sense a decaying mentality when a modern artist sees in the relic of the Grail and in sacred miracles the mission of German art, and proposes therewith to effect the regeneration of humanity.

Wagner's own utterances, and those of his associates and disciples even more so, speak for such a generalization of his newest ideal, just as Wagner's whole theory claims as a universal and exclusive fundamental of art only that which suits his own talent. Despite the efforts of a hundred Wagner associations to see the salvation of art in Christian mysticism, the present generation will hardly find it necessary to take up again Goethe's campaign against the 'new German religious-patriotic art'. We wish. . .to continue to live and work in the spirit of Goethe.[3]

Hanslick's second essay discusses the score; he preferred the second act to either of the others, but found the scene between Parsifal and Kundry musically cold and ugly. Here is his concluding paragraph:

And Wagner's creative powers? For a man of his age and of his method they are astounding. He who can create music as charming as the 'gambols of the flowers' and as vivid as the final scene possesses powers which our youngest composers may well envy. *Parsifal*, on the other hand, does not consist solely of such lucid intervals. It would be 'pure foolishness' to declare that Wagner's fantasy, and particularly his specifically musical invention, has retained the freshness and facility of yore. Once cannot help but discern sterility and prosaism, together with increasing long-windedness. Are not the irresistible Kundry's attempts at seduction rather stiff and cool in comparison with the similar scene in *Tannhäuser*? And is the Prelude to *Parsifal* not of the same origin and intent as the Preludo to *Lohengrin*? It is the same tree, but in one case in full bloom and in the other autumnal, leafless and chilly. Or compare the song of Gurnemanz in the 'Good Friday Spell' to the melodically related description of the Feast of St John in *Die Meistersinger*. . .Where is the inner strength, the singing soul of the model? Even the most powerful episodes from the *Ring*, considered individually and apart, have no equal counterparts in *Parsifal*, always excepting the chorus of the Flower Maidens, which stands quite alone. When one considers that those great moments in the *Ring* are distributed throughout four full evenings, the comparison may, to be sure, show a favourable balance. And *Parsifal* has the advantage of a more effective libretto. Although utterly inadequate as a 'dramatic poem', it is a better opera text. It is, in a word, more musical. If we regard it as a festive, magic opera, if we ignore, as we often must in any case, its logical and psychological impossibilities and its false religious-philosophical pretensions, we can find in it moments of artistic stimulation and brilliant effectiveness.[4]

In Hanslick's final essay, he saw no reason why *Parsifal*, 'like any other opera, played by professional singers in costume. . .for a continuously changing, paying public', should not be performed in theatres outside Bayreuth. 'One need not be a Wagnerite', he added, 'to complain in all sincerity of this threatened withholding of *Parsifal*. I know very well that Wagner is the greatest living opera composer and the only one in Germany worth talking about in a historical sense. . .But between this admission and the repulsive idolatry which has grown up in connection with Wagner and which he has encouraged, there is an infinite chasm.'[5]

Most early reactions were less measured than Hanslick's. Maurice Kufferath in his *Parsifal* (Paris, 1890), the most sensible of the few full-length books on the subject, summarized a representative selection of this 'indecisive and contradictory criticism. . .a curious mixture of in-complete judgements and cries of admiration'.[6]

The French music (as opposed to literary) critics were mostly close to Hanslick. Victor Wilder, in a long essay in the journal *Parlement*, praised the boldness of the text and the rigorous consistency of the score, but thought the work's 'mysticism' alien to modern sensibility. Saint-Saëns wrote in 1886 that 'any reasonably gifted young composer could produce without difficulty something a bit more seductive than the *Parsifal* duet'. But he had said to a friend in the Bayreuth audience: 'All the same, I wouldn't mind knowing how to do this, before doing otherwise.'[7] This respect for the scale of Wagner's genius was common to most of the French critics by now; with it went a justified fear that his influence would swamp the creative efforts of his younger contem-poraries. Edmond Hippeau in *'Parsifal' et l'opéra wagnérien* (Paris, 1883) wrote: 'One can admire Wagner when one reaches the real centre of his thought, but it is absurd to want, as the fanatics do, to make him the hub of the world, the alpha and omega of music, and to throw away the recognized masterpieces to replace them by this art which is an ex-ception.'[8] Hippeau was mocked by Kufferath for concluding: 'Wagner's work contradicts the French genius, which demands clarity, simplicity, abundance and variety of ideas',[9] but, as Georges Servières said in *Richard Wagner jugé en France* (Paris, 1887), 'the success of *Parsifal*, which, for many musicians, is Wagner's masterpiece, irritated French composers to distraction'.[10]

Kufferath shows that early opinion in Germany was more divided and unpredictable than in France. Paul Lindau in Berlin, like Hanslick, found Wagner's miracle-rich brand of Christianity, 'separated by centuries from our age of philological and historical research', repellent; Lindau was the first to read elements of anti-semitic fanaticism into the work.[11] By contrast, other German critics found the second act an immoral intrusion into a noble Christian work, while still others, again like Hanslick, thought the second act musically and dramatically the best. As Kufferath points out in the conclusion to this section of his book, many of these divergences sprang from the underlying conflict between two quite different aesthetic approaches: 'that which reduces all art to the level of a more or less agreeable entertainment' (Hanslick harking back to Goethe), 'and that which, finding in artistic sensibility the expression of man's highest aspirations, of the eternal Desire for the Best, makes art the complement of ethics and morality'.[12]

Wagner, of course, subscribed to the second view, and many objections to *Parsifal*, made both by his contemporaries and more recently, have come from those who have wished it possible to discuss *Parsifal* only from the premise of the first. Composers, and critics sharing Hanslick's anxiety for the musical tradition, have led this group. Debussy, for example, admired *Parsifal* greatly but regarded everything about it except the score as ludicrous. After two paragraphs of mockery aimed at the absurdities of the characters and plot, he concluded his note on *Parsifal* in *Monsieur Croche* (written 1903): 'The above remarks only apply to the poet whom we are accustomed to admire in Wagner and have nothing to do with the musical beauty of the opera, which is supreme. It is incomparable and bewildering, splendid and strong. *Parsifal* is one of the loveliest monuments of sound ever raised to the serene glory of music.'[13]

Sense, however, was not necessarily made of *Parsifal* by those who took it with full Wagnerian seriousness. The sentimental piety and weak intellectual grip of Francis Hueffer's pamphlet *Wagner's 'Parsifal': an attempt at analysis* (London, 1897) is typical of the feebleness with which English adulation of the work was generally formulated.

Clergymen and priests of various denominations have called *Parsifal* an *auto da fé*, an act of faith in a higher sense than applied to the sacred plays of Calderón; even those to whom the dogmas of Christianity are no longer a living thing could not fail to be impressed by the deep lessons of charity and pity and pure love which the poet has here taught, and of which all dogmas and symbolisms are merely the external embodiments. To this oneness of purpose he has indeed sacrificed dramatic possibilities of no mean order. The love-element is, for example, very prominent in the medieval treatments of the *Parsifal* myth. . .One can imagine how eagerly and other librettist would have grasped at these opportunities for 'love-duets' and other attractive situations; but Wagner passes on without heeding them. . .[14]

The *Revue wagnérienne* (Paris 1885-8) brought somewhat weightier forces than these to the discussion of *Parsifal.* The French literary Wagnerians included Edouard Schuré, who in 1885 wrote an unfavourable piece attacking the work for its implausibility and the uninspiring materialism of its religious content. His conclusions are much like Hanslick's, although reached by a different route:

Compared to the earlier works, the poetic conception of *Parsifal* lacks energy, consistency and clarity. If we explore the hidden content of the work, we find Schopenhauer's disciple. What is missing in this drama of compassion is the inspiration of hope, the sacred flame of the Christian religion and of all the great Aryan faiths. The feeble Grail, constantly threatened with extinction; the materialist theology of blood, devoid of any high spiritual feeling; the Redeemer paralysed by the sin of his earthly representatives — all this leaves a morbid impression barely concealed by the grandeur of the spectacle. Even in the music, beautiful though it is, there is more thirst for eternal rest than for eternal life, the active life of the soul and the spirit. The gnawing worm of pessimism has passed this way.[15]

And Schure ends by announcing that *Lohengrin* is in every way to be preferred to *Parsifal.*

Houston Stewart Chamberlain in the August issue of the following year came to *Parsifal*'s defence with an article which exceeded in overall comprehension and persuasiveness anything yet written about the work. (It is necessary to forget Chamberlain's later career as a vitriolic anti-semite and Nazi ideologue to give his early writing the credit it deserves.) The main strengths of the piece are its insistence on the length of the creative process which produced *Parsifal,* thus answering Schuré's charge of elderly exhaustion, and its illumination of the many parallels between *Parsifal* and *Tristan* and the *Ring,* which were being formed during the same period. He somewhat overstates these parallels, and does not mention *Die Meistersinger,* perhaps the most instructive comparison of all, but he ends with an attempt to define *Parsifal*'s relation to Christianity which at least brings the issue into something like the right focus.

It is unnecessary, after this historical account [of the work's creation], to state that *Parsifal* is not the glorification of a religious dogma. There is no more Christianity in *Parsifal* than there is paganism in the *Ring* or in *Tristan.* These three works, as we have seen, are contemporary; Wagner worked on them simultaneously; they are connected to each other by many imaginative links, and form for us — as they formed in the thought of the master — a whole. Wagner always recognized the bonds that unite Art and Religion; he never overstepped the frontiers that separate them. . .In 1880 he said: 'If someone asked me, "Do you want to create a religion?", I would answer that that is impossible; my ideas on this subject come to me only as a creative artist'. . .

In 1864 Wagner said: 'The most exalted work of art should replace real life, should dissolve reality in an illusion, thanks to which it would be reality itself which would appear to us as illusory. The nothingness of the world — here we would freely discover it, without bitterness, smiling!' And in 1882, in an article dated from Venice on 1st November and devoted to the memory of the *Parsifal* performances which had just taken place, he wrote: 'To forget in the contemplation of the work of art — a dream but true — the real world of falsehood, is reward for the sad truthfulness that forces us to recognize that the world is only suffering.' Nowhere in *Parsifal* do we touch the real world. We leave the 'realm of the Grail', where 'none but the innocent may come', and where the grace of the Grail alone feeds the faithful, only to enter the magic garden which Klingsor has 'made for himself in the desert' and filled with Flower Maidens. Once upon a time, Parsifal was to be seen doing nothing but wander through the world; now, this long section of his life, which filled the old poems, is reduced to a passing mention in the single line: 'Der Irrnis und der Leiden Pfade kam ich'.

In the *Ring* and in *Tristan* (which the master thought of as an act of the *Ring*) Wagner had created an image of real life, of 'the world which is only suffering': in *Parsifal* — where he intended, specifically, to set up exact parallels to the *Ring* — he 'constructed the holy world of a better life'.[16]

Chamberlain's assertion that *Parsifal* was not a Christian work did not go unchallenged. In the *Revue wagnérienne* of July 1888 Charles and Pierre Bonnier added to their earlier account of the Bayreuth production an analysis of the substance of *Parsifal* which discerned intelligently what may be described as Christian in the Schopenhauerian pessimism of the work.

In a word, Schopenhauer and Wagner see in Christianity, as in Buddhism, a representation of their philosophy. But for them it has nothing in common with popular religion. [Schopenhauer wrote:] 'The moral conclusions of Christianity are, in my opinion, explicable through the study of nature and are based on nature, whereas in Christianity they derive from childish stories.' And again: 'To make room for this principle of redemption, Christianity had to make use of mystical machinery, for example, the chalice which would save mankind.' Wagner wrote in 1880: 'What wrecked the Christian church was the assimilation of the divine being on the cross with the Jewish creator of heaven and earth; the joining to that angry God of vengeance the saviour of the poor who sacrificed himself for the love of all that is'.

In sum, Wagner and his Parsifal are Christians, but the story of

Parsifal and all its religious paraphernalia are only, to use Schopenhauer's phrase, 'mystical machinery' which represents for us the religion of Pity.[17]

These two paragraphs summarize with clarity the philosophical background which formed *Parsifal*'s unique relationship, as a work of art, to Christian belief and symbolism. No such summary can resolve all the problems raised by this relationship; these will be examined in the final chapter of this book. The *Revue wagnérienne*, however, provided a forum for the gradual transformation of critical reactions and impressions into reasoned assessments. Kufferath's book, the most thorough of the early accounts, made good use of these essays, particularly Chamberlain's (which Kufferath quotes at length and without proper acknowledgement). After a somewhat hesitant exploration of the theological penumbra of *Parsifal*, Kufferath follows the Bonniers' path through Schopenhauer's division of Christianity into good and bad components, and concludes with hopeful vagueness that 'in *Parsifal* Art has again become Religion', and that 'there is no other work of art which touches more directly on mankind's eternal problem, or which throws on our doubts and contradictions a more consoling illusion'. Meanwhile at one stage he has abandoned the Christian connection altogether, asserting that in Wagner's magnificent synthesis of the moral ideas of Schopenhauerian Buddhism, Kundry represents the Will to Live or Desire, Amfortas Suffering Born of Desire, and Parsifal Renunciation of Desire and therefore Peace in Negation.[18]

There are serious inconsistencies in Kufferath's argument but he makes in its course some interesting points that are entirely his own. The best example is the bond he finds between *Parsifal* and the works of other artists (and politicians) who grew up between the French Revolution and 1848. This passage makes odd reading. Knowing as we do that doom was gathering over Europe at the end of the nineteenth century, we may well feel that Wagner himself was more accurate when he described *Parsifal*, in the last passage quoted by Chamberlain, as an escapist work. But he wrote those gloomy phrases in 1882, when Germany had become the militarist and materialist empire of Wilhelm II. The point Kufferath is making refers back to the 1840s, the period of *Parsifal*'s conception, and it has a rival validity of its own. (The first two paragraphs show a surprising blindness to the deep correspondences that survive between Wolfram and Wagner — or perhaps Kufferath had not actually read Wolfram.)

The point on which Wolfram's poem turns is *doubt*. . .and the only philosophical message his work carries is to show us how Parsifal over-comes such doubt by the persistence with which, in spite of spiritual hesitations and wavering resolution, he pursues his goal, which is to be-come a perfect knight. This is, of course, the conception of a poet writing in the age when Church and chivalry most completely repre-sented the moral and social order, and when doubt as to the truths proclaimed by the church was considered the ultimate crime.

Wagner's moral theme is quite different. His hero is not for one moment a prey to religious uncertainty; he is no twelfth-century Faust. Parsifal is unaware of any kind of doubt; he passes through the world, that is, through the drama, without any anxiety over belief; on the contrary, all that matters to him is the life of the emotions. His simple, childish soul comes into being conscious only of its youthful energy and the strength of its desires, innocent to begin with of the world of feeling dormant within it, but entirely ready, through its purity and sincerity, to respond the more quickly to the first call of pity. Wagner shows us light dawning little by little in this soul, as it develops through the ordeals of harsh reality and rises, through compassion with every sorrow, to awareness of the divine. The idea of Redemption, outside any philosophical or religious system, is shown finally as identical to compassion, identical to the universal love to which humanity aspires, and which alone can put an end to the conflicts, oppression and crimes suffered by the world.

This is the fundamental idea. What Wagner borrows from the old tale thus turns out to be closer to us. For it should be noticed that this idea of Pity, of which *Parsifal* is the highest glorification in modern fiction, runs through all the literature of this century, set forth by the most various poets in the same sense as by Wagner. All Victor Hugo's work, to name but him, is full of this idea; and he is never nobler, more eloquent, more persuasive than when anathematizing anger and hatred and pleading for the humble, while evoking among the great deeds of the past or the present, the gentle image of Pity.

It is not only in literature, but in behaviour, social relations, even in political life, that a single, universal movement impelled people, during the whole of the first half of the century, towards a kind of general peace-making. Traditional quarrels between one people and another were suddenly extinguished; class hatreds disappeared; with an impulse of generosity, the best spirits wore themselves out looking for an amelioration of social injustice; even war was humanized. It was, in a word, as if a great breath of charity had passed over the old world and, just for a moment, brought us close to the ideal of primitive Christianity which proclaimed the equality of men against the pagan world and instituted the law of forgiveness and love.

Parsifal is nothing if not a magnificent hymn to this exalted feeling.

Wagner has often been reproached for choosing subjects outside common habits of thought, and for leaving on one side the general tendencies of the age. The reproach, besides carrying little weight, is ill-founded. *Parsifal*, which appears, on account of its mystical quality, to be a conception far removed from the present day, is in fact, of all modern works, the one which may be described as the most profoundly imbued with the spirit of the age.[19]

II

One can imagine the withering contempt with which Nietzsche, had he still been sane in 1890, would have greeted this rather sentimental effusion of Kufferath's. But he would not have disagreed with its last point. For Nietzsche was far from thinking, with Hanslick and many others, that the variety of Christian sentiment expressed or exploited — the distinction will concern us shortly — in Wagner's *Parsifal* was a nostalgic medievalism of no contemporary interest. It was precisely because he regarded *Parsifal* as the crystallization of all that was most degenerate and enfeebling in the world in which he lived that he seized upon it as the vindication of his own revulsion against Wagner.

For years of his youth Nietzsche had venerated Wagner as the only living great creative figure, and loved him as the father he had lost in childhood. By 1876 and the first Bayreuth festival, growing adulation of Wagner by the German bourgeoisie he despised, and a complicated personal resentment compounded with his own adoration of Cosima, was turning Nietzsche against his hero. In October 1877 he could still write to Cosima: 'The glories *Parsifal* promises us can comfort us in all the matters where we need comfort.'[20] At this point he knew only the 1865 prose sketch. By January 1878, when he received the full text from Wagner, he had already nearly finished *Human, All Too Human*, the book in which he rounded on his old friend with bitter and largely accurate attacks on Wagner's thirst for admiration, Cosima's self-sacrifice in the cause of her husband's egotism, and the unhealthy sycophancy surrounding them. The text of *Parsifal* was the last straw. Nietzsche added to his book such passages as this: 'But certainly frivolity or melancholy of whatever degree is better than romantic retreat and desertion of the flag, an approach to Christianity in any form; for in the present state of knowledge, no one can have anything at all to do with that without irredeemably besmirching his intellectual conscience.'[21]

As the years passed he more and more came to see the Christianity of *Parsifal* as the justification for what Wagner, now dead, had naturally regarded as a treacherous volte-face. In 1886 Nietzsche wrote, in a new preface to *Human, All Too Human:*

1876 was indeed high time to say farewell: soon after, I received the proof. Richard Wagner, apparently most triumphant, but in truth a decaying and despairing decadent, suddenly sank down, helpless and broken, before the Christian cross. Did no German have eyes in his head or pity in his conscience for this horrid spectacle? Was I the only one whom it *pained*?. . . As I proceeded alone I trembled; not long after, I was sick, more than sick, namely, *weary* — weary from the inevitable disappointment about everything that is left to us modern men for enthusiasm, about the universally *wasted* energy, work, hope, youth, love — weary from nausea at the whole idealistic lie and pampering of the conscience, which had here triumphed once again over one of the bravest. . .For I had had nobody except Richard Wagner.[22]

Wagner, he is saying, had betrayed him; therefore he had been compelled to abandon Wagner. In the following year, in the book *The Genealogy of Morals,* in which he elaborated his theory of master-morality and slave-morality, he took *Parsifal* as an extreme example of the life-denying menace of slave-morality. Asceticism, to the ill and celibate Nietzsche, was Christianity's most abhorrent ideal. Here he begins by hoping, perhaps half-seriously, that Wagner was only exploiting the religious connotations of *Parsifal*:

Is Wagner's *Parsifal* his secretly superior laughter at himself, the triumph of his ultimate artistic freedom, his artistic *non plus ultra* — Wagner able to *laugh* at himself?
    Clearly, one should wish that; for what would *Parsifal* amount to if intended as a serious piece?. . .A curse on the senses and the spirit in a single hatred and breath? An apostasy and reversion to sickly Christian and obscurantist ideals? And in the end even a self-abnegation, a self-crossing out on the part of an artist who had previously aimed at the very opposite of this, striving with all the power of his will to achieve the highest spiritualization and sensualization in his art? And not only in his art, but also in his life. . .
    Did the *hatred against life* become dominant in him, as in Flaubert? For *Parsifal* is a work of perfidy, of vindictiveness, of a secret attempt to poison the presuppositions of life — a *bad* work. The preaching of chastity remains an incitement to anti-nature; I despise everyone who does not experience *Parsifal* as an attempted assassination of basic ethics.[23]

Mock as he might, Nietzsche's feelings about Wagner remained as violent, and, one may suggest, *therefore* as mixed, as they did about Christianity. He continued to execrate Christianity, though he had long rejected its claim to be true, because for him Christianity was still a pole of his thought. At the end of *The Anti-Christ,* written in the autumn of 1888, he shrieked:

I *condemn* Christianity, I bring against the Christian Church the most terrible charge any prosecutor has ever uttered. To me it is the extremest thinkable form of corruption, it has had the will to the ultimate corruption conceivably possible. The Christian Church has left nothing untouched by its depravity, it has made of every value a disvalue, of every truth a lie, of every kind of integrity a vileness of soul. . .[24]

Yet, seven years before, he had written to a close friend: 'As for my attitude to Christianity, there is one thing you will surely believe: in my heart I have never really vilified it.'[25] Similarly, at Wagner's death in 1882, after years of furious estrangement, he wrote: 'Wagner was by far the *fullest* man I have ever known, and in this sense I have experienced a great deprivation these last six years', and: 'It was hard to be the enemy of the man one most reveres.'[26] And when in 1887 he heard the *Parsifal* prelude for the first time, he wrote, for all his virulent attacks of the same year:

Has Wagner ever done anything better?. . .there occurs in the very depth of this music a sublime and extraordinary feeling, a living experience and an event of the soul which does great honour to Wagner, a synthesis of states which many people, including our 'superior' intellectuals, will regard as incompatible: an awful severity of judgement 'from on high' which issues from an intimate understanding of the soul and sees through the soul, piercing it as with knives – and hand in hand with this goes a compassion for what has been perceived and judged. Only Dante is comparable, nobody else.[27]

This praise, of one incisive psychologist by another, was given in a private letter. The following year saw the completion of Nietzsche's love-hate relationship with Wagner in a new short book, *The Wagner Case,* and in an amended compilation from his earlier writings, *Nietzsche contra Wagner. The Wagner Case* is written with the dazzling brittle hardness of Nietzsche's last year of sane life: the glossy surface was soon to craze for good. In spite of the book's apparent lucidity, a deep ambivalence underlies its attack on Wagner, and on *Parsifal* in particular: as always, Wagner as Christian is the special object of Nietzsche's loathing. The book begins by contrasting Bizet with Wagner to make Wagner's religious and moral preoccupations look ridiculous:

You already see how much this music [*Carmen*] *improves* me? – *Il faut méditerraniser la musique.* . .The return to nature, to health, to gaiety, to youth, and to *virtue!* – And yet I was one of the most corrupt of the Wagnerians. I was capable of taking Wagner seriously. . .What a wise rattlesnake! All his life he has rattled before us about 'devotion', about 'loyalty', about 'purity'; with a panegyric on chastity, he withdrew from the *corrupt* world! – And we have believed him.[28]

The point, reinforced as Hanslick might have reinforced it, by the comparison of Wagner with Goethe, is to demonstrate that art should only entertain, and becomes ludicrous when it sets out to save:

What would Goethe have thought of Wagner? Goethe once proposed to himself the question, 'What is the danger which hovers over all romantics?' His answer was, 'Suffocation by chewing moral and religious absurdities over and over again'. In fewer words: *Parsifal*.[29]

There follows Nietzsche's famous attack on Wagner as a neurotic who has made music morbid, a stimulant for the decadent disguised as noble idealism and decked out with sham solemnity:

Let us never admit that music 'serves for recreation', that it 'cheers up', that it 'furnishes enjoyment'. *Let us never furnish enjoyment!* – we are lost, if people again think of art as hedonistic. That belongs to the bad eighteenth century. . .Let us choose the hour when it is suitable to look black, to sigh publicly, to sigh in a Christian manner, to exhibit large Christian sympathy. 'Man is depraved: who will save him? *What will save him?*' Let us not answer. Let us be careful. Let us struggle against our ambition, which would like to found religions. But nobody must venture to doubt that *we* save him, that *our* music alone brings salvation.[30]

Yet Nietzsche, just as he could not ignore Christianity, however often he asserted it to be false, could not rest his case against Wagner on the emptiness of Wagner's pretensions. He went on, thereby conceding that there was no cynicism in Wagner's use of Christian symbolic machinery, to take them as seriously as Wagner himself did. In his Postscript to *The Wagner Case* he judged *Parsifal* to be a real threat to truth and freedom, because, it should be noted, of its quality as a work of art.

Wagner is a seducer in the grand style. There is nothing fatigued, nothing decrepit, nothing dangerous to life and derogatory to the world in spiritual matters, which would not be secretly taken under protection by his art, – it is the blackest obscurantism which he conceals in the luminous husks of the ideal. He flatters every nihilistic (Buddhistic) instinct and disguises it in music, he flatters every kind of Christianity and every relgious form of expression of *décadence*. Let us open our ears: everything that has grown up on the soil of *impoverished* life, the entire false coinage of transcendence and another world, has in Wagner's art its sublimest advocate. . .His last work is in this respect his greatest masterpiece. *Parsifal* will always maintain the chief place in the art of seduction, as its *stroke of genius*. I admire that work, I should like to have composed it myself; not having done so, *I at least understand it*. . . Ah! this old magician! This Klingsor of all the Klingsors! How he makes war against *us* therewith! against us, the free spirits! How he humours every cowardice of the modern soul with Siren tones! – There was never such a *mortal hatred* of knowledge![31]

Nietzsche's argument is far from consistent. *Parsifal* is bad because art should merely entertain and not attempt to convey a message; *Parsifal* is simultaneously bad because the message that it conveys so well in fact corrupts. In the Epilogue to the book, Nietzsche has come full circle. Art should have a message, but it should be the message of self-affirmation, of master-morality and an anti-Christian insistence on this world's good and not the next's — as in the art, of course, of Goethe.

> If Wagner was a Christian, then Liszt was perhaps a Church Father! — The need of *salvation,* the essence of all Christian needs, has nothing to do with such harlequins; it is the sincerest form of expression of *décadence,* the most convinced and most painful affirmation of it in sublime symbols and practices. The Christian wishes to get *loose* from himself. . .Noble morality, master morality, has, reversely, its roots in a triumphing *self*-affirmation, — it is the self-affirming, the self-glorifying of life; it equally needs sublime symbols and practices, but only 'because its heart is too full'. All *beautiful* art, all *great* art belongs here: the essence of both is gratitude. . .I here remind you how Goethe, the last German of noble taste, felt with regard to the cross. One seeks in vain for more valuable, for more *indispensable* contrasts.[32]

So Nietzsche's mixed feelings persisted to the end: Christianity was a false account of the world, and Wagner was not allowed even to have held it to be true.

Nietzsche made no coherent critical assessment of *Parsifal*: he never heard the whole work and knew only the text and the prelude. But what he said about it is important, in the first place because his prophetic intellectual independence, together with his emotional dependence, give a unique interest to everything he wrote about Wagner; in the second place because his indecisiveness about *Parsifal* and its claim to be in some sense 'more than' a work of art has not even yet ceased to be influential. He pretended that Wagner might not have seriously held *Parsifal* to contain a saving significance; he knew, at the same time, both that Wagner was indeed serious and that the extra-aesthetic significance of *Parsifal* was, from his own point of view, to be deplored. Much uneasiness about the work, from that day to this, has sprung from a similar ambivalence.

Thomas Mann, consciously the heir of Schopenhauer, Wagner and Nietzsche on the one hand, and of Goethe on the other, was not free of this ambivalence, for all his Goethean insistence on the necessary unseriousness of Wagner as an artist. In his tremendous paper 'Leiden und Grösse Richard Wagners' ('Sufferings and Greatness of Richard Wagner'), given, in 1933, on the day before he left the Third Reich for exile, Mann praised *Parsifal* above all Wagner's works for its psychological acuteness, particularly in the character of Kundry, for its compelling use of its source material, and for its powerful unity of expression as the long-foreseen culmination of Wagner's whole creative career. But he denies Wagner's seriousness:

What is to be said. . .for the seriousness of that seeker after truth, that thinker and believer Richard Wagner? The ascetic and Christian ideals of his later period, the sacramental philosophy of salvation won by abstinence from fleshly lusts of every kind; the convictions and opinions of which *Parsifal* is the expression; even *Parsifal* itself − all these incontestably deny, revoke, cancel the sensualism and the revolutionary spirit of Wagner's young days, which pervade the whole atmosphere and content of the *Siegfried*. . .To the artist, new experiences of 'truth' are new incentives to the game, new possibilities of expression, no more. He believes in them, he takes them seriously, just so far as he needs to in order to give them the fullest and profoundest expression. In all that he is very serious, serious even to tears − but *yet not quite* − and by consequence, not at all. . .Among comrades the artist is so ready to mock at his own seriousness that Wagner could actually send the *Parsifal* text to Nietzsche with the signature: 'R. Wagner, Member of the Consistory'. But Nietzsche was no comrade. Such good-natured winking could not appease the sour and deadly, the absolute seriousness of his feeling against. . .Christianity. . .If Wagner by way of relaxation talked nonsense and told Saxon jokes, Nietzsche blushed for him. I can understand Nietzsche's embarrassment at this alacrity in moving from one plane to another; but something in me − perhaps fellow-feeling with Wagner as an artist − warns me not to understand it too well.[33]

By sleight of hand Mann here identifies Wagner with himself, and with his own ultimately ironic stance, in a league of creative artists whom poor earnest Nietzsche could not possibly understand. Mann's object, at a time when some of the prejudices Wagner had shared were bearing hideous fruit in Germany, was no doubt to de-fuse Wagner, to put him in a safe aesthetic category where his ideas could do no harm. Before the end of the same essay, however, Mann was back on Nietzsche's side, mourning the passing of true − i.e. Goethean − art. In his mocking and distancing description of *Parsifal* as a typically romantic bizarre concoction masquerading as a religious drama, Mann is at the same time conceding and laughing at Wagner's own serious intentions in *Parsifal*.

Great art may elsewhere too have succeeded in uniting the childlike and the elevated; but the combination of the extremely *raffiné* with fairy-story simplicity, the power to materialize − and popularize − the highly intellectual under the guise of an orgy of the senses; the ability to make the essentially grotesque put on the garment of consecration, the Last Supper, the bell, the elevation of the Host; to couple sex and

religion in an opera of greatly daring sex-appeal, and to set up that sort
of holy—unholy artistic establishment in the middle of Europe as a kind
of Lourdes theatre and miraculous grotto for the voracious credulity
of a decadent world — all that is nothing but romantic. In the classic
and humanistic, the really high sphere of art, it is quite unthinkable.
Take the list of characters in *Parsifal*: what a set! One advanced and
offensive degenerate after another: a self-castrated magician; a desperate
double personality, composed of a Circe and a repentant Magdalene,
with cataleptic transition stages; a lovesick high-priest, awaiting the
redemption that is to come to him in the person of a chaste youth; the
youth himself, 'pure' fool and redeemer, quite a different figure from
Brünnhilde's lively awakener and in his way also an extremely rare
specimen — they remind one of the aggregation of scarecrows in von
Arnim's famous coach. . .It is music's power over the emotions that
makes the ensemble appear not like a half-burlesque, half-uncanny
impropriety of the romantic school, but as a miracle play of the highest
religious significance.[34]

The swerves of direction in this great essay are no doubt partly at-
tributable to the political pressures under which it was written and
delivered. Five years later, in exile, Mann, wrote a calmer piece, on
Schopenhauer, which, while not mentioning *Parsifal*, discusses with the
utmost seriousness the ideas which give it dramatic life. He characterizes
Schopenhauer as a 'pessimistic humanist', and continues:

Since humanism in general is prone to rhetoric and the wearing of rose-
tinted spectacles, we have here something quite new, and, I venture to
assert, something in the realm of ideas considerably in advance of its
time. In the human being, the highest objectivation of the will, the will
is most brightly irradiated by knowledge. But in equal measure as
knowledge arrives at clarity, the consciousness is heightened, the
suffering increases, and thus in man it reaches its highest point. . .To
humanity alone is it given to achieve the final redemption, the renunciation of the will to live, as the artist mounts to the still loftier stage of
ascetic saintliness. To man is vouchsafed the opportunity to right the
wrong, to reverse the great error and mistake of being; to get the
supreme insight that teaches him to make the suffering of the whole
world his own and can lead him to renunciation and the conversion of
the will. And so man is the secret hope of the world and of all creatures;
towards whom as it were all creation trustfully turns as to its hoped-
for redeemer and saviour.[35]

Gurnemanz's words 'Das dankt dann alle Kreatur. . .' were surely in
Mann's mind when he wrote this passage, and no better summary of the
theme of *Parsifal* has ever been produced. The peroration of the
Schopenhauer essay seems, if Schopenhauer's ideas are accepted as the
chief inspiration of *Parsifal*, to concede everything that Wagner ever
claimed for his last work.

His pessimistic humanity seems to me to herald the temper of a future time. Once he was fashionable and famous, then half-forgotten. But his philosophy may still exert a ripe and humanizing influence upon our age. His intellectual sensitivity, his teaching, which was life, that knowledge, thought, and philosophy are not matters of the head alone but of the whole man, heart and sense, body and soul; in other words, his existence as an artist may help to bring to birth a new humanity of which we stand in need, and to which it is akin: a humanity above dry reason on the one hand and idolatry of instinct on the other. For art, accompanying man on his painful journey to self-realization, has always been before him at the goal.[36]

III

The greatly increased seriousness with which Thomas Mann in 1938 was prepared to entertain the central ideas expressed in *Parsifal* was in some measure due to Germany's rapid decline into barbarism in the preceding five years. There are few works of art so intricately involved in a country's history and fate as Wagner's have been: from early on, as we have seen, there were those, Nietzsche among others, to whom *Parsifal* represented the epitome of disastrous Germanness, and at the same time those who saw in it a flight from or an alternative to the brash satisfactions of the Wilhelmine empire. In any discussion of critical approaches to *Parsifal,* the part that it has been thought to play in political and social as well as cultural history cannot be left out of account.

In England such considerations did not, at least until 1945, excite much interest; nor, after the first naiveties, did the questions of how far and in what way *Parsifal* is a religious work. Partly as a result, there has until recently been very little English writing on *Parsifal* that could properly be described as critical. Newman gave a straightforward extended summary of the work in *Wagner Nights* (1949), but on the only occasion on which he attempted a critical judgement, in *Wagner as Man and Artist* (1914; revised 1924), he failed lamentably. He admitted to wishing that *Parsifal* had been a symphonic rather than a dramatic work, praised the music immoderately, rather as Debussy had done, and, for the rest, took refuge in an insecure jocularity.

We have outgrown the mental world of the work. . .The word 'redemption' has no meaning for me in the sense in which Wagner and the theologians use it. I can believe that redemption is a reality in the pawnbroking business; but if anyone tells me that men's souls are to be bought and sold, or lost and found again, without any volition of their own, I can only say that all this conveys about as much to my intelligence as talk about a quadrilateral triangle would do. . .The 'thesis' of a work of art is the one thing in it that does not concern us as artists. Who is to decide between rival philosophies or sociologies? Personally I believe that one philosophy is about as good as another, and worse. . . We had better leave alone the question of what the world would be like if we were to try to model it on *Parsifal*. . .[37]

After the Second World War, when Hitler's adoption of Bayreuth as the Nazi cultural shrine and the monstrous triumph of the anti-semitism to which Wagner had subscribed had involved Wagner's reputation inextricably with the German catastrophe, it was no longer possible to be blandly dismissive about the ideas in his work. The extreme denigration of Wagner as an effective force for evil was produced by an American, Robert Gutman, in his *Richard Wagner: The Man, His Mind and His Music* (1968). *Parsifal* is here seen as the comprehensive expression of whatever disreputable and crackpot ideas had taken the ageing composer's fancy, from anti-semitism to anti-vivisectionism. Gutman is compelled to ignore the length of the creative process which formed the work: this is his fundamental distortion, without which the whole fantastic structure of his vitriolic attack on *Parsifal* collapses. Some selective, but not unfair, quotation will give an idea of Gutman's blindness to ordinary considerations of logic and chronology. In his view *Parsifal* is a fanatical racialist tract tinged with homosexuality and demonism.

Surveying the world from the heights of Monsalvat, the Grail community in *Parsifal* was alarmed to observe natural selection working against its distinctive Aryanism. . .The knights were confronted with an enemy gaining upon them every day. Here was the decisive racial crisis that grew into an uncompromising struggle for power. *Parsifal*'s false facade of Christian abnegation masks this almost insane conflict. . .Amfortas contrasts the divine blood of Christ in the Grail with his own sinful blood, corrupted by sexual contact with Kundry, a racial inferior, this criminal miscegenation epitomizing the Aryan dilemma. . .The Grail and spear. . .are the fetishes worshipped in *Parsifal* and have nothing to do with the Jewish carpenter of Nazareth.[38]

Gutman sometimes misuses or misreads quotations. The agonisingly mixed feelings, temptation confusing the longing for salvation, described by Parsifal in his scene with Kundry, are not his own but Kundry's. Wagner did not call Klingsor the incarnation 'of the characteristic evil that brought Christianity into the world' but 'of the curious phenomenon which Christianity brought into the world: he does not believe in goodness'. This distinction is a subtle one; Gutman's conclusions are simple enough:

Even though *Parsifal*, more than the *Ring*, was the gospel of National Socialism, Wagner's genius operates on many levels, and. . .the work may also and more comfortably be regarded as his final treatment of the themes of empathy, growing awareness, and the love-death. But to be completely comfortable one must overlook the fact that, like Hans Sachs's benignity, the compassion extolled in *Parsifal* is restricted to a chosen group. . .The Third Reich overflowed with this particular kind of benevolence. *Parsifal* is not only un-Christian, it is anti-Christian. Nietzsche, who believed racial mixture to be the source of great cultures, recognized the opera as 'a work of malice. . .an outrage on morality'. Yet he also acknowledged the ingenuity of its libretto and the incredible beauty of its music. . .

In *Parsifal*, with the help of church bells, snippets of the Mass, and the vocabulary and paraphernalia of the Passion, Wagner set forth a religion of racism under the cover of Christian legend. *Parsifal* is an enactment of the Aryan's plight, struggle, and hope for redemption, a drama characterized not only by the composer's natively obscure and elliptical literary style, but also by the indigenous circumlocutions of allegory, the calculated unrealities of symbolism, and, especially, the sultry corruptions of decadence.[39]

There are signs here of three significant weaknesses in Gutman's case. In the first place, Gutman makes considerable use of Nietzsche in the course of his argument. Yet Nietzsche regarded *Parsifal* as bad because it was Christian, not because it was anti-Christian; and, if 'the gospel of National Socialism' is in question, most people would consider Nietzsche's reduction of all motives to the will to power, his contempt for the weak and his ruthless revaluation of values to have contributed more to Nazi brutality than did Wagner's *Parsifal* ideas of saving pity and renunciation. What is more, the fact that Hitler held a certain view of a work of art should not necessarily be thought to make that view the correct one. In the second place, *Parsifal* can only be described as 'obscure and elliptical' and full of 'circumlocutions' and 'unrealities of symbolism' if its plainly stated meaning is being ignored in favour of another, imposed meaning. Gutman says: 'In *Parsifal* little is directly named by the mysterious text or elusive motifs, and the audience is left to divine meanings.'[40] What is going on in the work is, on the contrary, though far from simple, made quite clear, both in the text and in the score; but Gutman's interpretation has little connection with either. In the third place, and most importantly, Gutman's revealing concession about Nietzsche's acknowledgement of 'the incredible beauty' of the music suggests a fault in his approach which is confirmed shortly afterwards when he says:

It remains an enigma of genius that Wagner was able to yoke all this bizarre paraphernalia embracing the catalogue of his neuroses to both an allegory of the fallen and redeemed Aryan and a symbolic representation of the developing human soul, to overlay the whole with a rather cheap and cracking veneer of fake Catholicism, and yet achieve a monumental masterpiece.[41]

That Wagner conceived and executed his works as dramatic wholes should by now be axiomatic. It is not critically possible to separate the text from the music and to call the second sublime and the first pernicious rubbish; such attempts, Newman's being a mild and Gutman's a wild example, are certain to fail, and to convey in the end a clearer picture of the critic's prejudices than of the work's qualities. To regard *Parsifal* as vicious rather than ridiculous is, however, at least to take it seriously.

A third possibility, a curious mixture of the serious and the unserious characteristic of late twentieth-century criticism, is to regard *Parsifal* as interesting but harmless, as an entertainment or *jeu d'esprit* on however solemn a level, a closed system of expertly revolved symbols. This has been in recent years the most frequent critical means of dealing with *Parsifal*. It neutralizes the demands the work makes and renders it acceptable to generally held atheist realism. An elaborate mythical interpretation, such as that put forward by Werner Diez in his essay 'Prometheus, Lucifer and the Utopia of the Grail' (1972), would so firmly connect *Parsifal* to familiar works of art of the past as to categorize its problems out of existence. In Diez's view, Klingsor and Amfortas are descendants of a single 'mythological source-figure', Lucifer—Prometheus, with Klingsor inheriting Lucifer's attributes and Amfortas Prometheus's, both being in tormented revolt against Zeus— God—Titurel. Klingsor—Satan exercises black magic in opposition to Titurel's white magic; only Parsifal, 'the Utopian man', is free of the power of either kind of magic and will inaugurate 'a future humanity' on the ruins of both.[42] This account is less far-fetched than Jacques Chailley's book of 1979, *Parsifal: Opéra Initiatique*, which sets out to prove *Parsifal* to be a conscious and consistent Masonic work. But Diez's lack of a qualitative distinction between Greek and Christian mythology is no less un-Wagnerian. His description of the powers of Klingsor and the Grail as equally balanced magical fields, between which Parsifal must thread his way, is derived from Wieland Wagner's celebrated *Parsifalkreuz*. This diagrammatic 'psychological pattern', which appeared in the programme book of the 1951 Bayreuth festival, is an impressive demonstration of the symmetries in character and incident in *Parsifal*, and no doubt helped Wieland Wagner to organize the austere groupings of his revolutionary production. But its very neatness closes off many possibilities of response.

'It follows', Wieland Wagner noted at the bottom of his diagram, 'that there must be absolute similarity between Kundry's fate and that of Amfortas, as well as between the "white" magic of Titurel and the "black" magic of his opponent Klingsor.'[43] This tidy pattern-making, like Wieland Wagner's 1966 description of *Parsifal* as depth psychology ('What does depth psychology aim at? To interpret, clarify, sift'),[44] is in fact a sterilizing process of translation. Wagner does not in *Parsifal* – as perhaps he does in the *Ring* – present black magic and white magic as equal forces to be overcome by his hero. Instead he presents evil and good, in idiosyncratic and unexpected manifestations, and Parsifal's triumph is unequivocally the victory of the good. Demands for agreement, and not only for emotional sympathy, are thus made on the audience, and to state the possible views of *Parsifal* as simple exclusive alternatives, as Wieland Wagner did in 1966, is to seek to dodge those demands: 'Depth psychology plays a great part in *Parsifal,* and is the human explanation of the plot and the characters. For the public at large, however, *Parsifal* remains a Christian mystery play.'[45]

A more sophisticated confinement of *Parsifal* within the safe quarantine area of the aesthetic is achieved by Carl Dahlhaus, the most judicious of contemporary Wagner critics. The chapter on *Parsifal* in his *Richard Wagners Musikdramen* (1971; English translation 1979) is one of the most illuminating short accounts to be found anywhere. But its introduction, in support of the view Dahlhaus elsewhere expresses as 'Art was the only idea in which Wagner believed', confuses rather than clarifies some difficult issues:

Wagner's faith was philosophical, not religious, a metaphysic of compassion and renunciation, deriving its essential elements from Schopenhauer's *World as Will and Idea* and – via Schopenahuer – from Buddhism. Wagner found these elements also present in Christianity, and to that extent he was a Christian. But the predominant spirit of the nineteenth century had become alien to fundamentalist faith, and he too took a historico-philosophical view of the traditions of the religion as an evolving truth, changing its outer shape throughout history. The myth that was once believed as literal truth had become a metaphor for a metaphysical insight; and the rituals of an earlier age, grown hollow and insubstantial as such, passed over into art, so as to preserve or recover in a symbolic role the meaning and cogency that they had lost in their hieratic function. In 1880 Wagner wrote in *Religion and Art*, the philosophical complement to *Parsifal*: 'One could say that where religion is becoming artificial it is for art to salvage the nucleus of religion by appropriating the mythic symbols, which the former' — religion in its mythic phase — 'wished to propagate as true, for their symbolic worth, so as to reveal the truth buried deep within them by means of ideal presentation of the same.' *Parsifal* is therefore undeniably a document of the nineteenth-century 'religion of art'. This does not mean that art should be venerated as religion — or as pseudo-religion, for the holder of fundamentalist Christian views — and works of art worshipped as religious icons, but that religion — or its truth — has passed from the form of myth into the forms of art. The historico-philosophical hour had come for the art that, in Wagner's view, was the quintessence of all the arts: drama.[46]

This paragraph, particularly in the 'therefore' of the antepenultimate sentence, slides over the crucial question of whether or not 'the truth' in which Wagner believed and which he thought of as buried within the outworn symbols of Christianity has or has not, for him or anyone else, an existence outside those symbols and beyond the art (*Parsifal*, for example) which he saw as taking their place. If it has, dangerous questions of belief are raised, as Nietzsche realized. 'Compassion and renunciation', for instance, are not in themselves 'a metaphysic' but moral imperatives backed by beliefs requiring commitment. As Nietzsche in revolt against Schopenhauer rightly showed, they do not 'work' in rational terms. *Parsifal* is no straightforward religious drama referring to the commonly recognized framework of institutional Christianity. It is something else, something that would never have come into being without what Dahlhaus calls 'Wagner's faith'. But to distinguish between philosophical and religious faith so that the former — which Dahlhaus allows Wagner — appears acceptably neutral and realist ('historico-philosophical') and the latter — which Wagner is said not to have had — appears unacceptably partisan and ideological is misleading. Schopenhauer explained the truth as he saw it in order that converts might be won to it from falsehood: he demanded belief, not mere assent to rational argument. This is the area in which *Parsifal* exists: if, as Dahlhaus rightly says, Wagner reckoned the truth of religion to have passed into the forms of art, it is still truth, as well as art, that is at issue.

In a later (1972) and even better short account of *Parsifal*, Dahlhaus simplifies his view of the part played by Christianity in the work, now seeing it as no more than nostalgic:

It is on the sensation of being led back into the past by the music that the significance of the religious element in *Parsifal* depends. Christianity — seen as sacramental religion and not diluted and reduced to the condition of a philosophical abstraction — belongs to the past, according to the belief which Wagner gives expression to in the music. This is why the Last Supper celebrated on the stage during the Grail episodes of *Parsifal* is less a re-enaction — which would be in questionable taste — than a memory transformed into a picture. Wagner's *Bühnenweihfestspiel* does not absorb the rite it evokes by making it real and living, a religious ceremony presented through the medium of art, but by revealing it as belonging to the past, as a form that no longer carries any substance, a vision called up from the depths of memory.[47]

Here the frequent aim of consigning the religious elements in *Parsifal* to a safe aesthetic distance has been particularly attractively achieved. The argument is made all the more persuasive by its context, in which Dahlhaus gives an excellent account of *Parsifal* as music drama at its purest, the 'background' of interior development, symbolic significances and the entanglement of past and present playing a far greater part than the 'foreground' of the visible action.

Dahlhaus's assessment of *Parsifal* is probably the most widely acceptable account yet given. His description of the score, and of the particular expressive devices which distinguish *Parsifal* from Wagner's other works, could be expanded but not improved upon. Yet his confinement of the religious component of the work to mere personal 'philosophy', or to a cleverly evoked but dead past of 'fundamentalist faith', leaves some important problems unconfronted.

Michael Tanner, an English philosopher, has recently faced these problems anew in his essay 'The Total Work of Art' (*The Wagner Companion*, 1979), the scale of his conclusions being appropriately large although their correctness is open to question. Tanner sees *Parsifal*, as Dahlhaus and Wieland Wagner in their varying ways also do, as a masterpiece remarkable for its self-contained coherence as a work of art. But he does not neglect its further demands, its underlying insistence on assent to a truth outside itself. The kind of truth he takes this to be, however, is suggested by his final bracketing of Wagner with Nietzsche, Freud and Lawrence as 'figures who may even now give us hope, if there is hope to be had'; and this orientation slants his description of *Parsifal* at many points. Of Amfortas's arrival in the first scene he says: 'In the miraculously blooming phrases surrounded by ravishing wind solos and a wonderful stillness, we have a sense of what nature can do, without any aid from "Supernature" ', and continues:

As Amfortas speaks of his relief, he is surrounded by a halo of beauty, but a halo that is entirely *immanent*; and that makes my basic point about the whole wonderful work. The radiance that streams from it, as well as the sometimes frightening agonies of spirit, come from within the characters and their natural settings; only at one or two uncertain moments does Wagner betray what is unquestionably his central insight and allow something transcendent to appear, causing momentary embarrassment – the solo voice at the end of Act I. . .and the dove at the end of the whole work.[48]

Tanner's method of distancing the Christian element in the work is to say that *Parsifal,* rather than being a religious work, is *'about* religion'. Thus:

The first act, complex as it is, is set out in such masterly orderliness by Wagner that it should not present interpretative problems; but as soon as we try to see *Parsifal* as a 'religious work', it presents nothing else: for everything seems either irrelevant, blasphemous or banal. But seen as the most penetrating study we have of the psychopathology of religious belief in artistic terms, it is an incomparably involving experience.[49]

This reference to psychopathology may remind us of Mann's neurotic crew of misfits. Unlike Mann, however, Tanner does face the problem of describing the religious belief actually portrayed in *Parsifal,* but his account of it turns out to be an imposed and arbitrary delimitation. Here is his version of the work's climax:

The supreme dramatic moment, of course, is Gurnemanz's anointing of Parsifal with ointment, and as King. What follows, the so-called 'Good Friday Music', is not a chance for Wagner to extend himself lusciously over a lovely theme, but is of crucial significance. For it is as soon as Parsifal has been anointed that he notices for the first time the beauty of the meadows and flowers, no longer seductive or even, for the moment, sustaining, but simply existing, at rest and radiant. Wagner is at his most daring here, but. . .he has rendered his message into terms so headily sensuous that attention is diverted from the extraordinary words of Gurnemanz:

> Wie des Erlösten Leiden du gelitten,
> die letzte Last entnimm nun seinem Haupt!

(As you have endured the sufferings of the redeemed one, now lift the last burden from his head!)

I have no doubt that Robert Raphael is right when he says that Parsifal, 'having now redeemed himself by insight and empathy, symbolizes a Christ who *does not have to die,* but lives' (*Richard Wagner* 1969 p. 121). The point about not having to die is that Wagner, like many people, is repelled by the idea of the Second Person of the Holy Trinity dying in order that the First Person should allow man into Heaven. He is impatient, in fact, with the transcendental, though as a late child of the Christian era he found it a handy mythology for expressing his own idiosyncratic, indeed epoch-making insights. But once having got Christ down from the Cross, or rather stopped him getting on to it, Wagner reinforces his anti-transcendental redemptivist vision by directing our attention to Nature, to what, at the climax of the 'Good Friday Music', Gurnemanz refers to as. . .'all that lives and soon must die'. It is in *entsündigte Natur* ('transfigured Nature') that Parsifal will find what he has been looking for *beyond* Nature; for when Gurnemanz tells Parsifal that it is Good Friday, Parsifal breaks out into bitter lament, but is corrected with ineffable gentleness, and Gurnemanz stresses that 'All creatures now rejoice', because – and here the point is made again – 'No more can Nature see Him Himself on the Cross: it looks up to redeemed mankind'. Wagner achieves here the most remarkable balance; while Nature has never been painted in more exquisite colours, it is none the less no longer, in its unconscious loveliness, a temptation: it looks up to man who, in transcending Nature, has no need to transcend himself.[50]

If it is accepted that it is Christ who is addressed by Gurnemanz in the first couplet quoted, that 'absolved from sin' rather than 'transfigured' is the correct translation of 'entsündigte', and that the connection between Good Friday and the crucified saviour is in any way retained by Wagner, this argument falls to pieces. Tanner's final statement of his interpretation is uncompromising:

Parsifal demonstrates how in detranscendentalizing Christianity it is possible to find value in a world not created and governed by incomprehensible Goodness and Power.
A last point about *Parsifal*: in the greatest art there has always been transmitted a sense of some fundamental inscrutability, and it has normally been attributed to Fate, or God, or the gods, or to something external to man. And tragedy, where inscrutability tends to be given its head, has often been thought to be the expression of some final element of the ineffable at the heart of things: we are condemned always to remain in darkness about what matters most. But increasingly in the modern age, with the collapse of Christianity and the rise of the novel and of music-drama, inscrutability has been relocated as being in the heart of man. Going with that relocation is the faint hope that we might finally become less opaque to ourselves and to each other. One way in which that could happen would be by understanding better the art of Wagner, and above all of *Parsifal*.[51]

We are back, in fact, with psychology. The question that arises, not only from Tanner but from almost all the modern, liberal writing on *Parsifal* since Mann became a modern liberal, is this: does *Parsifal* really re-locate inscrutability in the heart of man? Or, to put the same question differently, can *Parsifal* rightly be seen as showing forth nothing stranger than psychology – the 'hope that we might. . .become less opaque to ourselves and to each other'? Was Nietzsche, then, simply mistaken to see in *Parsifal* 'the entire false coinage of transcendence and another world'; and was Wagner after all of Nietzsche's party without knowing it? A tentative answer will be given in the next chapter.

6 *A proposed interpretation*

This fine poem has something of the nature of a riddling ballad in which the symbols are suggestive and resonant beyond the sense of any single interpretation, and in which the movement is through layer after layer of mystery to the heart of the matter, satisfyingly disclosed at the end so that it illuminates the whole poem.

Note on the Corpus Christi carol, *Medieval English Lyrics,* ed. R. T. Davies, p. 364

Critics, starting with Wagner himself, have always had difficulty with the classification of *Parsifal.* Wagner invented the awkward term *Bühnen-weihfestspiel* − 'festival play of consecration' − to distinguish the work from his music dramas (a term which, of course, he had earlier invented to differentiate them from operas). The kind of resistance put up to this distinction, or, rather, to the assertion it contains that *Parsifal* is in some class by itself, is often indicated by the alternative, wider genre proposed for the work. Hanslick recommended his readers to regard it as 'a superior kind of magic opera', and some later spectators, whether inclining to a Masonic interpretation or not, have come to similar terms with it as a heavyweight *Magic Flute.* The reverential, who fiercely resist management's invitations, including Wieland Wagner's at Bayreuth, to applaud all three acts, are treating its performance as a quasi-liturgical event. Tanner and Dahlhaus, because of the interior location of the drama in Parsifal's head, see it as quintessential music drama, although Dahlhaus, pointing out the passivity of the hero, also says it is 'close to being an example of that paradoxical genre, the hagiographic drama'. Liszt was struggling with the genre problem when he wrote: 'It would be an odd contradiction to admire the last scene of *Faust* Part II and to excommunicate *Parsifal.* . .Many poets known to be religious and Catholic strike me as coming nowhere near Wagner's level of religious feeling.'[1] Mann, on the contrary, placed *Parsifal* as the extreme 'roman-tic' work set over against Goethe's 'classic and humanistic, . . .really high sphere of art', and regarded its 'religious significance' as a trick

129

6 Wolfgang Wagner's set for Act I Scene 1; Bayreuth 1975—

played on the audience's emotions by the music.

A tangle of confused assumptions surrounds this question of the genre to which *Parsifal* belongs. We no longer live, and for some three centuries have not lived, in what Leavis called 'the world of Dante or of Herbert'. Nevertheless, whether we are Christians or not, we all know, or think we know, the difference between sacred and secular works of art. While pictures, poems, pieces of music, stay within these categories, we receive them from prepared positions that do not have to be thought out on each occasion. An atheist can hear a sacred piece by Stravinsky or Britten with as little philosophical fluster as a Christian can, or as either can hear the B Minor Mass. Both will order their responses differently if the work is being used liturgically. This, of course, *Parsifal* cannot be: its eucharistic scenes are strictly representational, paintings not icons. But this ease among the categories depends upon the properties of the sacred remaining fixed and known, a set of terms and images which together form a description of the world and human life that some regard as sufficient and most reject or ignore as wishful delusion. If the stability of these terms and images is upset by some dynamic enterprise of creative enquiry that transcends the familiar categories, engaging within the secular the old shapes of the sacred, and not just as nostalgic reminiscence, we lose our bearings and are forced to react with a fresh and strenuous attention. *Parsifal* is such an enterprise, and the nature of an appropriate response to it is suggested in Leavis's remarks on another such work, Eliot's *Four Quartets*:

That the poetry seems to invite a given intellectual and doctrinal frame may be found to recommend it. But the frame is another thing (and the prose is not the poetry. . .). The genius, that of a great poet, manifests itself in a profound and acute apprehension of the difficulties of his age. Those difficulties are such that they certainly cannot be met by any simple re-imposition of traditional frames. Eliot's. . .poetry is remarkable for the extraordinary resource, penetration and stamina with which it makes its exploration into the concrete actualities of experience below the conceptual currency; into the life that must be the *raison d'être* of any frame – while there's life at all.[2]

If it is accepted that *Parsifal* is indeed such a work, forcing the avoidance of the swift label and the critical short cut, the term *Bühnenweihfestspiel* may be accepted also, not for its elegance, but for its announcement of oddness. Wagner is in it requesting our disregard of categories that no law of logic or taste maintains, but only habit.

All Wagner's mature works are hybrids: his adulteration of music with extraneous content in the interests of drama is the distinguishing characteristic of his music dramas, as opposed to other composers' operas. *Parsifal* is, further, a hybrid also in its mixing of the sacred and secular aesthetic categories. In its most successful scenes these various conflations function with marvellously sustained elaboration. In the two scenes between Kundry and Parsifal, where Parsifal is in Kundry's emotions confused with Christ almost to the point of identity, but in neither his own nor the audience's emotions confused with Christ at all, Wagner, by the intensely skilful and subtle use of words and music, brings off the most complex passages of his 'festival play of consecration' without a jolt. The same is true of the scene between Klingsor and Kundry, where the crossing of the categories produces the particular quality of Klingsor's imprisonment in cynicism as the obverse of a Christian good. But the character of Amfortas, and the Grail scenes of which he is the centre, are less successfully achieved, and the reason for this is to be found in another, and this time a too strained, conjunction.

The trouble lies in Wagner's omnivorous use of his sources. In Wolfram to some extent, and certainly in the pagan Celtic penumbra of legend on which he drew, the wounded Fisher King is a figure of impaired magic power, whose impotence is responsible for the dereliction of the waste land he rules. His wholeness, and the health of his kingdom, are to be restored by the fairy-tale asking of the right question; the Grail is no more than the most important element in his magical entourage. In the later, fully Christianized Grail stories, on the other hand, the wounded king recedes to become a mere element in the entourage of the Grail, which has advanced to its place as the most potent symbol of Christ's continuing presence in the world. In Malory, for example, the Maimed King is indeed healed by Galahad in the Grail's proximity, but he vanishes from the story to become a holy monk; the guardian of the Grail and celebrant of its eucharistic rite is Joseph of Arimathea in the likeness of a bishop. Wagner, by keeping as essential parts of his plot both the pagan force of the wounded king whom the hero from afar must heal and the Christian force of the Grail which itself will heal the pilgrim hero, has set up, as it were, two rival fields of energy.

Although the seamless texture of the music very largely conceals their collision – the opening motive, in particular, unites in one complex of anguish the suffering of Amfortas and of Christ both at the Last Supper and in the Grail deprived of its power – there is an unresolvable friction in their juxtaposition. In the first Grail scene, for example, the eucharistic hymn from the dome praises the saviour:

> Der Leib, den er zur Sühn' uns bot,
> er lebt in uns durch seinen Tod.

> His body, which he offered for our sin,
> lives in us through his death.

Titurel tells Amfortas that he may be absolved from sin in serving the Grail; and Amfortas himself cries out for mercy to 'the All-merciful' – 'Du Allerbarmer! Ach, Erbarmen!'. But because, according to the other, magical version of these events, which Wagner is simultaneously presenting, Amfortas must wait for Parsifal to bring him redemption, the redeeming Grail of this strongly invoked sacramental theology has to be kept in unforgiving powerlessness until Parsifal's journey is over. Amfortas's sin and repentance, in other words, belong to a different story from Amfortas's unhealed wound, although the sexual guilt with which Wagner binds them together is a triumphant psychological and dramatic invention. By keeping both, however, and also because of the temporal requirements of a staged drama, Wagner is forced to devise a piece of plot machinery found in none of his sources, the pressure from Titurel and the other knights that compels Amfortas to perform his office. The element of cruelty produced by this device in the first Grail scene is much more obvious in the second. Here the magic power of the Grail to sustain its retinue is deeply confused with the Christian power of the rescued Grail to heal and reconcile. The results are that the threatening knights of the one story, determined to keep the cult in being for their own sake, jar badly with the kind, sad Gurnemanz of the other story; the hounding of Amfortas, repentant but unforgiven, seems too cold and fierce to be reconciled with the warmth and light of the work's conclusion; and Parsifal's summary curing of Amfortas's wound seems weakly predictable compared with the long resolution of his relationship with Kundry in the preceding scene.

But some of the inconsistencies here, and also in other parts of the work, go beyond the clash between pagan and Christian Grail stories held by Wagner in uneasy balance. For Wagner, through these same characters and actions, is telling a third story also, the Schopenhauerian–Buddhist story of renunciation of the will and redemption through compassion. Perhaps surprisingly, this theme sorts better with the pagan than with the Christian elements in the Grail material Wagner used. The reason is that, in both the pagan heroic rescue and the Schopenhauerian renunciation, human virtue alone is necessary, whereas Christian salvation involves the real power of the divine. It is therefore the character of Parsifal that bears the brunt of these incompatible versions of events. Amfortas may be caught between the magic of one kind of healing and the sacramental redemption of another, but he is only the recipient of Parsifal's Schopenhauerian compassion. Parsifal, on the other hand, within whom the central crisis of the work takes place, has to be both providentially drawn to the Grail and its conscious rescuer, both the object of grace and a resolute Kundry-withstanding subject, both redeemed and redeemer, both Christian patient and Schopenhauerian agent, for in Schopenhauer's scheme of things there is no God. Here, in this much more profound conflation of different — and, one might suppose, mutually exclusive — interpretations of life, Wagner is astonishingly successful. So successful is he that it may easily escape the critic's notice that there are conflicting ideas at work here at all. It may well appear to those more familiar with Schopenhauer than with Christianity that the recommendation of human compassion and denial of the will is indeed the ultimate theme of *Parsifal*. Such an assumption lies behind Tanner's firm assertion of Wagner's 'anti-transcendental redemptivist vision', and also behind Dahlhaus's eloquent insistence that 'according to Wagner's conviction, Christianity belongs to the past'. Nietzsche, apostate child of a long line of Lutheran pastors, thought differently.

That Schopenhauer's redemption through denial of the will from the circle of conflict and suffering is in fact incompatible with Christian redemption from sin through grace may perhaps be disputed. Are they, it may be asked, any more than different ways of talking about the same thing? The answer is that they are indeed more; and that the crucial difference between them is that whereas, for the Christian, salvation comes from God through Christ, for Schopenhauer it is a purely human achievement won through perception of the grim realities of existence, leading to renunciation of the individual will to life. *Meistersinger* which, for all its radiance, has at its centre the story of just such an achievement, is Wagner's most fully Schopenhauerian work. No one would put it into the category of sacred art. *Tristan*, on the other hand, more obviously Schopenhauerian in its headlong course towards 'the wide kingdom of the world's night', has been called, by Joseph Kerman in *Opera as Drama*, 'a religious drama'. The argument with which he supports this description has an instructive bearing on *Parsifal*.

Kerman takes his definition of religious drama from Una Ellis-Fermor's account of *Samson Agonistes*, and applies it to *Tristan*:

The fundamental sense is of a progress towards a state of illumination which transcends yearning and pain. The fundamental rhythm of the piece is towards Tristan's conversion and the concluding *Liebestod* of Isolde — a triumphant ascent, not a tragic catastrophe. And *Tristan*, I believe, meets three other conditions that Miss Ellis-Fermor would wish to apply to religious drama. The nature of the experience is properly religious; the experience is the main matter of the drama; and the religious experience is actually, paradoxically, projected in a dramatic form. . .The extraordinary conception slowly and surely grips the audience: love is not merely an urgent force in life, but the compelling higher reality of our spiritual universe.[3]

After his persuasive analysis of the third act of *Tristan*, Kerman concludes that the work has 'a final conviction' which 'the later operas somehow lack', and compares it with certain Bach cantatas in which 'like Wagner in *Tristan*, Bach deals centrally with religious conversion, the awareness and agony of sin, the acceptance of the Passion, and the final submersion in the universal'.[4]

Kerman's comparison of *Tristan* with Bach cantatas reveals a casualness in the treatment of varieties of belief which undermines his use of the word 'religious'. There is in his eyes no qualitative difference between the beliefs expressed in *Tristan* and those expressed by Bach: both are 'religious' because both produce 'a state of illumination which transcends yearning and pain'. What has happened here is that Wagner, through the tremendous creative pressure which gives *Tristan* its compelling unity and consistency, has transformed a bleak and negative philosophy into a positive affirmation whose force persuades Kerman that it can be called religious. Schopenhauer regarded the will to life, of which he called sexual passion the most extreme manifestation, as evil, the universal conflict it produces as the cause only of suffering, and its denial as the way not to happiness but to a lessening of pain. This rigid and élitist pessimism Wagner transmutes into an assertion of temporary and subjective clarity and bliss on the edge of oblivion. Neither in Schopenhauer's negative and general, nor in Wagner's positive and particular vision, can this conception of the world, without wilful distortion of the adjective's ordinary meaning, be called religious. 'Religion' implies an element of submission to the divine, and also an element of goodness in such submission. *Tristan* conveys neither. One has only to change Kerman's 'love' to the more accurate 'sex' to see that this is so.

To *Parsifal*, on the other hand, Kerman's genre label 'religious drama' does apply, although − or because − it lacks the unity of *Tristan*. In *Parsifal* the presence of the divine is established through the symbol of the Grail, whose power draws Parsifal to itself. At first he is incapable of understanding this summons to grace, and the growth in knowledge that leads to his submission is also a growth in goodness. It is therefore true to say of *Parsifal*, as it is not of *Tristan*, both that the hero's conversion is the work's central subject and that 'the nature of [this] experience is properly religious'. It is also, as it happens, properly Christian, even if its Christianity is sometimes overlaid by remnants of Schopenhauer which Wagner saw no more cause to expunge than remnants of pagan magic.

Amfortas, locked into a cycle of suffering caused by his yielding to sexual passion, is a victim of the will to life ('my Tristan of the third act, with an inconceivable increase'). Klingsor, on the other hand, who has forcibly dissociated himself from sexuality by his self-castration, lives in a world of sin comprehensible only in religious terms: he has sought to attain the divine by a fraudulent route and his cynicism has brought him a power which goodness instantly destroys. Kundry has been punished for her Schopenhauerian crime of *Schadenfreude* — also a Christian sin against love, in the person of Christ — by her total subjugation to sexuality: her own repentance, by which she will pass back to the realm of love (the tenderness of Parsifal's reconciling kiss), can be released only by another's denial of the will. Parsifal, in whom these contradictions are at their most acute, must be the blameless Schopenhauerian renouncer, capable of understanding the pervasive evil of the will and withdrawing himself from its sway. Yet he cannot receive the redemption of Christian forgiveness unless he is also conscious of his own sin. This he is, not only in the early stages of the third act, before his own salvation is complete ('Und ich, ich bin's, der all dies Elend Schuf!': 'And I, it is I, who am the cause of all this misery!'), but at the moment of revelation produced by Kundry's kiss, the pivot of the whole work, when knowledge and guilt strike him simultaneously. He understands at the same instant Amfortas's suffering and his own neglect of the Grail's need for rescue, and falls to his knees crying:

> Erlöser! Heiland! Herr der Huld!
> Wie büss ich, Sünder, meine Schuld?

> Redeemer! Saviour! Lord of grace!
> How may I, a sinner, atone for my guilt?

That Parsifal should be redeemed and guilty at the same time, as he is by the third act, is a familiar Christian paradox, 'simul iustus, simul peccator', in Luther's phrase, incomprehensible only if the Christian dimension of the work is ignored.

The truth is that Wagner, for all his passionate discipleship of Schopenhauer, had never entirely abandoned the Christian promise of redemption which transforms with hope the despairing description of the world Schopenhauer had inherited from the Christian past. A fine passage on Burckhardt and Schopenhauer in Erich Heller's *The Disinherited Mind* puts very well the relation, highly relevant to *Parsifal*, between Schopenhauer and Christianity: Burckhardt, Heller says, like Schopenhauer,

> may have abandoned the belief that the offer of redemption reached man in the shape of an historical event and was rejected by a creature bent on the *continuation* of his history. But, again like Schopenhauer, he accepts an *order of things* identical with that accepted by the Christian believer. It is the only order of things in which the religion of Christ can make sense, and if it is the *true* order of things, it is, at the same time, a profoundly *senseless* pattern *without* the religion of Christ. To look upon man, as Schopenhauer and Burckhardt did, as the fallen creature, on sin and evil as constituent and ineradicable factors in human history, on human affairs as pathological, without believing in the reality, existence, possibility and indeed the definite offer of spiritual health, must needs create a profound spiritual predicament. . . This predicament they bore nobly, and with a strength of spirit and character which is rare among human beings.[5]

One does not have to accept Villiers de l'Isle Adam's story of Wagner's unequivocal assertion of Christian belief in 1868 to recognize that the stoical pessimism described here was not his view of the world. If the nature of 'the possibility of spiritual health' is left undefined in *Meistersinger* and the *Ring*, its presence is nevertheless clear, and in *Parsifal* it has become the 'definite offer' of Christian redemption. Nor is this, as Nietzsche thought it, an elderly relapse from courageous realism. The creative world of *Parsifal* — each of his works inhabited a separate region of Wagner's mind — had always been Christian. In April 1857, in his most Schopenhauer-obsessed period, a spring morning in Zürich had revived the memory of Wolfram and prompted the first sketch: 'Out of my thoughts about Good Friday, I rapidly conceived a whole drama.'[6] Eight years later, and a few weeks before the first performance of *Tristan*, he wrote to Ludwig:

> Today it is once more Good Friday. O holy day! Most deeply significant for the world! Day of redemption! God in suffering – who can take in the tremendous scale of it? And yet, even as it lies beyond words, so it is the closest thing of all to mankind. God the Creator – he must remain entirely beyond the grasp of the world; God the loving guide – he can be inwardly loved, but not understood; but God the sufferer – he writes himself in our hearts with fire; this tremendous anguish washes away the stubbornness of life. To see God in suffering! The teaching that we cannot take in now takes hold of us: God is in us – the world is vanquished. Who created it? Useless question! Who overcame it? God in our

hearts — the God that is grasped in the deepest pain of fellow-feeling.[7]

This is profoundly Christian in impulse and understanding (and expressed in prose whose quality far exceeds that with which Wagner is usually credited: the play on 'begreifen' and 'ergreifen', to take in, take hold of, is particularly striking). It foreshadows the complicated relation in *Parsifal* between the power of the Grail to save man and the Grail's need to be preserved by man. In 1873, while working on the score of *Götterdämmerung,* Wagner wrote, also to Ludwig: 'Parsifal. . . will be the crown of my whole creative endeavour. . .It seems to me as if the making of this work has been entrusted to me in order to uphold to the world its own most profound mystery, the truth of the Christian faith; indeed, even to rekindle this faith.'[8] And in 1882 his last words on *Parsifal,* in the passage which Chamberlain (cheating by translating *Abbild* as *oeuvre d'art*) quoted as evidence of pure aesthetic escapism, actually confirm this diagnosis:

Who can look, through a lifetime, with an open mind and a free heart on this world of murder and theft, organized and legalized by lies, deceit and hypocrisy, without from time to time turning away from it in horrified disgust? On what then do we turn our gaze? Most often on the void of death. But to him on whom a different call is made, to him who is picked out by fate, there then appears the true picture [*Abbild*] of the world, as a premonition from his innermost soul foretelling redemption. To forget before this picture, which is a dream of truth, the real world of falsehood, seems the reward for the sad truthfulness which has forced him to recognize the misery of the world. Can he after this help himself in the formation of this picture with further lies and deceit? You must admit that this would be impossible.[9]

Wagner, this passage demonstrates, could not ultimately support the senseless evil and suffering of the world as the whole and only truth, but turned towards a vindicating truth set over against it, which not only reveals its evil as evil and its lies as lies, but redeems man from their power. However obscurely and unphilosophically Wagner here expresses it, there is a logic in this position — in the sense that evil can be recognized as such only from a belief in the existence of good — which Schopenhauer, who saw the will to life as evil but recognized no countervailing good, simply ignored. Nietzsche's clarity would not allow him this swerve of the mind: hence his view of the 'will to power', his version of the force that drives the world, as morally neutral, and his realization of the need to create a totally new system of values (his attempt to meet this need contributed, at least, to the final breakdown of his sanity). Not that Nietzsche was without grief for the past. One of his saddest and most terrifying sentences runs: 'Error has transformed animals into men; could truth be capable of transforming man again into an animal?'[10] But his commitment to this stark and value-deprived truth made him see Wagner's position as only a cowardly turning back towards illusion. And *Parsifal* was more than mere assuaging diversion (Nietzsche also said: 'Truth is ugly. We possess *art* so that we *shall not perish of truth.*'[11]). *Parsifal* revealed not a dreamy concealment of unendurable truth in consoling clouds of fantasy but commitment to a cancelling truth, to the unique, irreducible, demanding offer of redemption which Christianity declares.

Here we have reached what must be the crucial point in any critical discussion of *Parsifal.* It is easier, perhaps, to decide with Chamberlain, Dahlhaus, Tanner and many others that Wagner uses the trappings of Christianity only to exploit the symbolic charge they retain from the past; that it is not only possible but correct, since 'Art was the only idea in which Wagner believed' (Dahlhaus), to sit through a performance of the work without feeling to any degree threatened or persuaded by the ideas it embodies. But although to reject this purely aesthetic approach is to plunge into the far deeper water of actual belief, actual truth, this is the demand that *Parsifal* does make — in fact and not only in Wagner's intention. In case it is doubted that the complicated problem of the relation between poetry and belief has any relevance to *Parsifal,* Heller's note to his essay on Rilke and Nietzsche may help to define the area in which, I suggest, *Parsifal* belongs:

Where beliefs embodied in poetry are as important as they are in what one may call confessional poetry, we cannot fully appreciate the poetry without being at least *tempted* to accept the beliefs as well. With such poetry before us, complete immunity from infection would prove either the bluntness of our perception or the worthlessness of the poetry.[12]

As Leavis said in *The Living Principle* about the Eliot of *Four Quartets*: 'It is obviously not enough to say that [he] applies a major poet's genius to expressing intense personal conviction. In such an undertaking, what he offers is offered as having general validity.'[13]

In order to decide whether or not this is so in the case of *Parsifal,* it is necessary to assess the degree and quality of specific Christian conviction that it does embody. In what follows the words and music are regarded, no less than elsewhere in this commentary, as inseparably connected in the attainment of a single expressive purpose. Because of the intrinsically verbal and referential character of Christian belief, however, the words — the theological interpretation that Wagner himself gives us — are here of primary importance.

The Grail in *Parsifal*, for all the bits and pieces of pagan legend that Wagner retained, demands to be taken in its full Christian sense as the perpetually renewed chalice of the Last Supper which represents Christ's continuing presence among men. If it is not so taken, many of the words used to describe it and its place at the centre of the drama, itself needing redemption from the plight to which Amfortas's failure has brought it, become meaningless. The Grail's need for rescue informs the whole of Gurnemanz's gradual imparting of information in the first and third acts. It is the cause of the guilt that strikes Parsifal at the moment of Kundry's kiss:

> Des Heilands Klage da vernehm ich,
> die Klage, ach! die Klage
> um das entweihte Heiligtum:
> 'Erlöse, rette mich
> aus schuldbefleckten Händen!'

> The lament of the Saviour there I now understand,
> the lament, ah the lament
> from the profaned sanctuary:
> 'Redeem, rescue me
> from guilt-defiled hands!'

And, at the very end of the work, it is the preservation of the Grail which is celebrated in the closing words of the chorus: 'Erlösung dem Erlöser!' ('Redemption to the Redeemer!').

The idea that Christ's continuing presence in the world depends, in some sense, upon Christian fidelity is a sound intuition (the church as the body of Christ is an orthodox formulation of it). It is the idea expressed by Wagner not only in the Grail's need for faithful service but also in Gurnemanz's Good Friday explanation, in the words:

> Ihn selbst am Kreuze kann sie nicht erschauen:
> da blickt sie zum erlösten Menschen auf. . .

> [The created world] cannot see the Saviour himself on the cross:
> it looks up to man redeemed. . .

Un-Christian, on the other hand, indeed almost anti-Christian, is Wagner's requirement — some of the time — of total sinlessness (Schopenhauerian will-lessness) in those who have charge of the Grail. Parsifal, however, in spite of all we are told of his purity and of the path to the Grail being unfindable by sinners, is keenly aware of his own sin, and of his implication in the general sinfulness that hides the Grail. It is his repentance and forgiveness, associated with Kundry's, that form the dramatic core of the Good Friday scene, and Gurnemanz's prayer over him is Christian in the fullest sense, is accompanied by a tremendous assertion of the Grail theme, unclouded by doubt, in the orchestra, and is followed at once by Parsifal's baptism of Kundry to the words:

Die Taufe nimm
und glaub' an den Erlöser!

Receive this baptism
and believe in the Redeemer.

The baptism is accompanied by the music signifying faith, now equally specific in application.

The Good Friday scene, Parsifal's arrival at the goal of his journey and both his and Kundry's liberation from the past, strikes most people as the work's true climax. The scene is both written and composed with a sureness of touch and a quality of conviction that the final Grail ceremony, confused by an incompatible clutter of dramatic require- ments, does not have. It is surely significant that it is in the Good Friday scene that the Christian strand in the complex texture of the drama predominates. Kundry's deliverance from a Schopenhauerian—Buddhist cycle of suffering into mortality is also a deliverance from lust into love and from remorse into penitence and therefore forgiveness. Parsifal moves from the forlornness of his quest through a storm of contrition to the healing of Gurnemanz's absolution, in which Christ is invoked as the source of the power to heal. And in Gurnemanz's marvellously composed hymn to the wonders of Good Friday, it is possible to hear Wagner's lifelong search for a believable shape — a *wahrhaftigste Abbild* — of redemption coming to an at last sufficient conclusion.

Nietzsche railed against the Christianity he found in *Parsifal* on the grounds on which he railed against Christianity in general: he regarded belief in God as a devaluation of the human, and belief in the transcen- dent as a denigration of mortal life and of the earth. 'Everything that has grown up on the soil of *impoverished* life, the entire false coinage of transcendence and another world, has in Wagner's art its sublimest advocate.'[14] In *Twilight of the Idols,* written in the same year as *The Wagner Case* postscript, he said: 'A Christian who is at the same time an artist *does not exist. . .*Raphael said Yes, Raphael *did* Yes, consequently Raphael was not a Christian.'[15] An appreciation of Nietzsche's view of Christianity is perhaps commoner nowadays than an appreciation of Christianity (the former colours, for example, Tanner's account of *Parsifal,* which he greatly admires, as 'antitranscendental'). It cannot be too strongly stressed, however, that, however widely disseminated it has become, Nietzsche's view of Christianity was partial, prejudiced and in important respects inaccurate. In the value which, through its understanding of the incarnation, Christianity gives to the human, the mortal, the created, it is, as a system of belief, at its furthest remove from Buddhism and Schopenhauer. Of the doctrine of the incarnation Nietzsche had no grasp at all: it negates his whole picture of Christianity. Wagner, on the other hand, shows in *Parsifal* an instinctive sense of the central importance of the incarnation, the most fundamental distinguishing mark of Christianity as a religion. The arbitrary, single, transforming fact of God become man and therefore flesh, of the transcendent assuming a physical, tangible presence in the real world, is, of course, the background of the whole Grail myth in its Christian form. Wagner, using the myth as the substance of a late nineteenth-century music drama, does not, for all the other conflicting material he uses, in the end betray this essential significance.

In Wolfram, the Grail, although only a stone, has a deeply reverberant Christian resonance. The stone is called 'the most precious thing of paradise' and then 'the most precious thing of all the earth'. Only a chaste maiden was allowed to bear (sic: the German word is 'tragen') the Grail; she carried it past an old man kept alive in order to see it. Its name is *lapis exilis* which may be a corruption of *lapis ex caelis* ('stone from heaven'), or may mean 'small stone' from a source Wolfram used which tells of a small stone from Paradise too heavy for mortals to move but weighing, when covered with dust, nothing at all.[16] The echoes raised by all this would have been clearly heard by Wolfram's thirteenth-century audience. Wagner uses none of it in *Parsifal*; nevertheless in the whole work, and particularly in his Good Friday meadow, he retains to a remarkable degree the sense of the incarnation as the vindicating fact which redeems the real world not by devaluing it in relation to the transcendent but by involving it with the transcendent and so giving it new value.

Leavis, in his classic analysis of *Four Quartets* in *The Living Principle*, dissents from the beliefs offered in the poem because of their assertion of the absolute otherness of the transcendent, and because of the unresolved conflict between this assertion and Eliot's own creative grasp of the actual. From a long and subtle argument it is possible here to quote only fragments:

In *Four Quartets*, for all the creative energy devoted to establishing the approach to apprehending, the painfully developed or enforced offer of apprehension is illusory: the real to be apprehended is nothing. It is the postulated otherness, the only relation to which that can be conceived. . .is one of conscious utter abjectness, utter impotence, utter

nullity. . .
In fact a conception of pure non-human otherness can hardly be a conception; it can be no more than the ghost of one – a mere postulate. The space cleared for the Other by the elimination of all that 'human kind' can recognize as life, value and significance is a vacuum, nothing is left to qualify it.[17]

This, more carefully and coolly put, is Nietzsche's case against *Parsifal* (no accident, this, since Lawrence, Leavis's standard of judgement in many ways, was a true Nietzschean), except, of course, that Leavis is too scrupulous to regard the attack on a Christian poem as thereby an attack on Christianity. One could put his criticism differently by saying that in the Christianity of *Four Quartets* the sense of the central importance of the incarnation is lacking: there is no evocation of the transforming presence of the transcendent – Christ – in the real, mortal world, and hence the real, and particularly the individual human being, is left without value. Or, as Leavis says, the transcendent is left without reality: 'No transcendental apprehension is convincingly imparted, because the life of the meaning insists on belonging to what figures as metaphor – that is, to the this-world actual of human existence and experience; to the life to which Eliot denies value.'[18]

If Wagner had presented his Grail as untethered metaphor, as a symbol whose meaning was locked into itself, this would be equally true of *Parsifal.* But his allowance of its full, Christian, transcendental reference to the Grail has the result that it successfully imparts both a sense of the divine and a sense of the presence of the divine in human existence and experience. That of which the Grail is a symbol is that to which Parsifal, Kundry and Amfortas must answer for their sin, and also that which, once Parsifal has released it from the confusion (dust) of its betrayal by Amfortas, will free them from their sin. To quote Leavis once more: 'There is no acceptable religious position that is not a reinforcement of human responsibility.' And, conversely: 'Unless it has a religious quality the sense of human responsibility can't be adequate to the plight of the world that so desperately needs it.'[19]

With this last remark Leavis begged large questions which he never answered. They were questions which haunted Wagner all his life; because he was a dramatist he both posed them and approached their resolution by means of particular characters and situations. The burden of responsibility which, in their different ways, Sachs and Wotan each carry, is compounded of experience, knowledge and culpability for the disorder which has overtaken the community they also have the power to set to rights. This power, paradoxically, lies in renunciation; they must yield their own will to life, in particular their own impulse to love, and so transfer to a new hero, young and innocent, the load that has exhausted them. 'We must learn *to die,* and to die in the fullest sense of the word', Wagner wrote, commenting on the *Ring,* to Röckel in 1854. 'The fear of the end is the source of all lovelessness.'[20] The pathos of this renunciation, delayed in each case by an outburst of passionate regret, affected Wagner so deeply that, in the lengthy formation of *Meistersinger* and the *Ring,* his sympathy for the burdened master overtook his initial emphasis on the bold youth, and Sachs and Wotan replaced Walther and Siegfried as the central figures of the drama. In the course of *Parsifal*'s evolution, Wagner saw this same process — the replacement of the hero by Amfortas as the character of principal interest — looming as a danger before him, and avoided it by exactly following his own prescription: 'Parsifal's development must be brought back to the foreground.'

So effectively is this achieved that Amfortas may well be felt as, in the end, an insufficient counterweight to the hero. Parsifal, in the completed work, takes on the dramatic force of both innocence and wisdom: he travels all the way from light-hearted ignorance, through the kind of knowledge that Walther and Siegfried experience only as delight, to renunciation and the successful re-ordering of the disrupted community. It is he who, like Walther and Siegfried, must be initiated by an intermediary woman into adulthood and the pull of sex, but it is also he who, like Sachs and Wotan, must achieve the restoration of order through superior knowledge and love and the renunciation that they demand. For this reason it is a mistake to regard Parsifal, as Dahlhaus does, as 'a passive hero'. The very structure of the drama clearly demonstrates that he is the instigator of the action: in each act his arrival breaks into a static situation as the new element that will change everything. In the first act his healing power as the prophesied fool is only promised: he is not yet wise and must leave again. In the second act he irrupts into the circle of malice and despair that binds Klingsor and Kundry together in eternal hatred, and shatters it. In the third act, where the parallel and contrast between the stupid boy who is questioned by Gurnemanz and throws down his bow and the weary knight who is questioned by Gurnemanz and heavily lays down his arms is perfectly drawn, he comes to transform dissolution into new integrity.

Parsifal's growth, from his shooting of the swan to his return of the spear, is a growth in responsibility. Because of the presence and reference of the Grail, this responsibility has an explicit religious quality not present in the *Ring* or *Meistersinger.* While we know what Wotan and Sachs are responsible *for,* what they are responsible *to* is far from clear. Wotan on the slope of Brünnhilde's rock, greeting his unconscious heir across cosmic distances and the lost Wälsung generation, is saving himself from the destructive impulses of ambition and love; Wagner's haverings over the ending of the *Ring* show that whatever else Wotan is saving remained for his creator in a limbo of uncertainty. Sachs resigning Eva to Walther in the intimate surroundings of his beloved town is preserving the natural succession of youth to age and, in his lesson on the rules of singing, handing on the discipline without which inspiration cannot find consoling form. The consistent drive of each drama makes us feel that these acts of renunciation are good. But in *Parsifal* Wagner undertakes a harder task: to present, in the symbol of the Grail, goodness itself, the absolute sanction which both justifies and requires the renunciation made in its favour.

We have here approached a level of abstraction alien to Wagner's methods. In the actual texture of the drama he expresses the symbolic power, and temporary weakness, of the Grail in three ways (which can be separated only for the purposes of argument). Visually, the representation of the Grail ceremony draws its meaning from the eucharistic connotations which the director must allow it to evoke: without them it becomes a merely magical device too feeble to fill its central place in the drama. The dove which appears at the work's conclusion must, similarly, have the quality of mysterious benediction that it had for Wolfram; if its age-old resonance as the symbol of the Holy Spirit (as, for example, in Piero della Francesca's *Baptism of Christ*) is entirely missed, it becomes a property of painful irrelevance. Musically, the Grail, in the variously broken and mended chords of the Dresden Amen, is established in the score with consummate success as the offered possibility of healing which also needs, itself, to be healed. Its supreme moment of restoration is not in the final scene but in Gurnemanz's prayer over the absolved Parsifal, now anointed as king. Verbally, the promptings supplied by Wagner towards the audience's sense of the Grail vary from slight and untheological hints (Gawan's unlicensed departure at the very beginning; the knights in Act III forced each to find his own food in the absence of the Grail's sustenance) to the resounding statements of external meaning which form the dramatic hinges of the work. Obvious examples are Parsifal's understanding of the Grail's plight at the moment of Kundry's kiss, and his baptism of the penitent Kundry with the words: 'glaub' an den Erlöser' ('believe in the Redeemer'). A less obvious but no less important example is Gurnemanz's command to the silent, exhausted Parsifal:

Schnell ab die Waffen!
Kränke nicht den Herrn, der heute,
bar jeder Wehr, sein heilig' Blut
der sündigen Welt zur Sühne bot.

Lay down your arms!
Do not offend the Lord, who today,
lacking all weapons, offered his healing blood
in expiation for the sinful world.

It is at these words that Parsifal thrusts the spear into the ground, lays down sword, shield and helmet beneath it, and kneels to pray. Here, and in all the ritual actions which follow — Kundry's washing and anointing of his feet, Gurnemanz's sprinkling and anointing of his head — Parsifal must not be seen as Christ, the Redeemer, but only as a man redeemed, who nevertheless carries the responsibility of revealing Christ's continuing redemptive power to the world which 'Ihn selbst am Kreuze kann sie nicht erschauen'. The distinction is of the utmost importance.

Without the steadily maintained Christian frame of reference within which Act III Scene 1 takes place, Parsifal would be, as he has seemed to many, a kind of *ersatz* Christ, a substitute figure put through some of the motions of the story of Jesus by a cynical, or just a late, dramatist, too sophisticated to put Christ himself on the stage. Within the frame, however, Parsifal becomes the representative man that Christianity declares anyone potentially to be: a sinful man redeemed by Christ who can and should at the same time disclose the reality of Christ to others. This is a theological, and an incarnational, idea of some complexity, which Wagner, again, probably grasped more by instinct than from study. It is, however, not inappropriate to gloss the Good Friday scene with a quotation from St Paul:

It was God who reconciled us to himself through Christ and gave us the work of handing on this reconciliation. In other words, God in Christ was reconciling the world to himself, not holding men's faults against them, and he has entrusted to us the news that they are reconciled. . .For our sake God made the sinless one into sin, so that in him we might become the goodness of God.[21]

Wagner presents this idea, of course, through the opaque medium of his drama: the psychological interplay of Parsifal, Amfortas, Kundry and Klingsor keeps it at one remove from the audience — until Gurnemanz in this climactic scene several times directly refers to it. And it is the very exteriority of the idea which makes it properly Christian: what Gurnemanz tells Parsifal in the passage just quoted is, precisely, 'the news' which explains and justifies all that he has experienced.

Parsifal shares with Sachs and Wotan their paradoxical mixture of power and powerlessness: a knight who lays down his arms as a sign of victory, he also knew that the sacred spear was not a weapon to be used in ordinary battle. By adding to this paradox a Christian description of it, Christ's own reversal of values, Wagner brought his life's work to a conclusion that was as surprising against the background of general nihilism so lucidly discerned by Nietzsche as it was in the context of the palely liberal theology then being taught in Germany. Thirty years ahead of Karl Barth's revolution, Wagner had produced a music drama which, among other things, carries a foretaste of that return to dynamic theology. Barth wrote in 1916:

Knowledge of God is not an escape into the safe heights of pure ideas, but an entry into the need of the present world, sharing in its suffering, its activity and its hope. The revelation which has taken place in Christ is not the communication of a formula about the world, the possession of which enables one to be at rest, but the power of God which sets us in motion.[22]

These sentences are as good a description as any of the genuinely Christian impulse in *Parsifal.*

For all its inconsistencies and occasional lapses into the banal (the martial chorus of the first act, the Flower Maidens, the knights' bullying in the third act – all to weak passages in the score), *Parsifal* is, finally, created in the service of a greater truth. To the extent that the spiritual certainty to which it refers is thought to belong to the past, it will seem nostalgic, embarrassing, unhealthy, quaint, boring: and people will be driven to explain its beauty, if they find it beautiful, by separating the words from the music and ignoring the words. But to the extent that the spiritual certainty to which it refers is still thought, whether from within or from without, to have an incontrovertible experiential force, it will seem at once humbler, braver and more worthy of respect for the encouraging light it sheds upon the tormenting questions of real, human, life.

In a remarkable passage of *The Disinherited Mind,* Heller brilliantly and rightly turns the impoverishment argument against Nietzsche:

Without that all-pervasive sense of truth which bestows upon happier cultures their intuition of order and reality, poetry − in company with all the other arts − will be faced with ever increasing demands for ever greater 'creativeness'. For the 'real order' has to be 'created' where there is no intuitive conviction that it exists. The story of the rise of the poet from the humble position of a teller of tales and a singer of songs to the heights of creation, from a lover of fancies to a slave of the imagination, from the mouthpiece of divine wisdom to the begetter of new gods, is a story as glorious as it is agonizing. For with every new gain in poetic creativity the world as it is, the world as created without the poet's intervention, becomes poorer; and every new impoverishment of the world is a new incentive to poetic creativeness. In the end the world as it is, is nothing but a slum to the spirit and an offence to the artist. Leaving its vapours behind in audacious flight, his genius settles in a world wholly created by the creator−poet. . .Neither Rilke nor Nietzsche praise the praiseworthy. They praise. They do not believe the believable. They believe. And it is their praising and believing itself that become praiseworthy and believable. . .Theirs is a *religio intransitiva*.[23]

In spite of the scale of his creative genius the Wagner of *Parsifal* does not belong with Rilke and Nietzsche. He had − almost in his own words − an intuitive conviction of the existence of the 'real order'; his praise and his belief in *Parsifal* do have an object; and the Good Friday scene is the most moving of all modern celebrations of, precisely, 'the world as created without the poet's intervention'.

The almost uncanny sympathy which Wagner had for the Grail story, and for the mixture of sexual yearning, wandering, sadness and healing repentance that make of Act III Scene 1 of *Parsifal* one of his very greatest achievements, is shown by the late medieval English carol which he cannot have known, for it was not printed until 1907:

> Lully, lullay, lully, lullay,
> The falcon hath borne my make away.
>
> He bore him up, he bore him down;
> He bore him into an orchard brown.
>
> In that orchard there was an hall,
> That was hangéd with purple and pall.
>
> And in that hall there was a bed
> It was hangéd with gold so red.
>
> And in that bed there lieth a knight,
> His woundés bleeding day and night.
>
> By that bed's side there kneeleth a may,
> And she weepeth both night and day.
>
> And by that bed's side there standeth a stone,
> Corpus Christi written thereon.[24]

[*make*: mate; *may*: maiden]

If this simple, anonymous little poem, from the world of 'tellers of tales and singers of songs', mixes the sacred and the secular in a knot we find hard to untie, so, and in the same way, though with elaborate and conscious subtlety of technique, does *Parsifal.* So also does Christianity, for the distinction belongs to art, not to life.

Notes

Except where specified all translations are my own.

1 The sources

1 *Richard Wagner an Mathilde Wesendonk,* ed. W. Golther (Berlin, 1904) p. 243.
2 *Ibid.* p. 146.
3 Wolfram von Eschenbach, *Parzival,* trans. H. M. Mustard and C. E. Passage (New York, 1961) p. 1.
4 *Ibid.* p. 177.
5 *Ibid.* p. 210.
6 *Ibid.* p. 431 (I have altered the translation).
7 *Ibid.* pp. 126−7.
8 R. Wagner, *My Life,* anonymous translation (London, 1911) p. 617.
9 R. Wagner, *Sämtliche Werke,* vol. XXX, eds. M. Geck and E. Voss (Mainz, 1970) p. 12.
10 Fragment (music and words), quoted in E. Newman, *Wagner Nights* (London, 1949) p. 663.
11 *Richard Wagner an Mathilde Wesendonk,* pp. 52−3.
12 *Ibid.* p. 110 (this letter is wrongly dated 2 March 1859).
13 *Ibid.* p. 148.
14 *Ibid.* pp. 243−4.
15 Eschenbach, *Parzival,* p. 405.
16 *Ibid.* p. 318.
17 R. Wagner, *Prose Works,* trans W. Ashton Ellis, vol. VIII (London, 1899) p. 315.
18 *Richard Wagner an Mathilde Wesendonk,* p. 242.
19 R. Wagner, *Letters* (The Burrell Collection) ed. J. N. Burk (New York, 1950) p. 657.
20 The Brown Book sketch is printed in full in R. Wagner, *Sämtliche Werke,* vol. XXX, pp. 68−77.
21 Eschenbach, *Parzival,* p. 131.
22 *Ibid.* p. 67.
23 R. Wagner, *Sämtliche Werke,* vol. XXX, pp. 18−19.
24 C. Wagner, *Diaries,* trans. G. Skelton, vol. I *1869-1877* (London, 1978) p. 944.
25 *Ibid.* p. 860.
26 *Ibid.* p. 861.
27 cf. Max Unger, 'The Cradle of the Parsifal Legend', *Musical Quarterly,* vol. XVIII, 1932, pp. 428−42.

28 R. Wagner, *Gesammelte Schriften und Dichtungen* (2nd edn, Leipzig, n.d.) vol. x, pp. 172–3.
29 C. Wagner, *Diaries*, trans. Skelton, vol. I, p. 947.
30 *Ibid.* p. 984.
31 C. Wagner, *Die Tagebücher*, eds. M. Gregor-Dellin and D. Mack, 2 vols. (Munich, 1976-7) vol. II, p. 60.
32 Eschenbach, *Parzival*, p. 408.
33 *Ibid.* p. 411.

2 Text and synopsis

1 C. Wagner, *Die Tagebücher*, vol. II, p. 214.
2 The note is printed in R. Wagner, *Sämtliche Schriften und Dichtungen* (Leipzig, 1911) vol. XII, p. 347.

3 The music

1 C. Dahlhaus, *Richard Wagner's Music Dramas*, trans. M. Whittall (Cambridge, 1979) p. 151.
2 See in particular the third essay in C. Dahlhaus, *Zwischen Romantik und Moderne* (Munich, 1974; trans. M. Whittall as *Between Romanticism and Modernism*, California Studies in 19th Century Music, Berkeley, 1980). See also A. Schoenberg, *Theory of Harmony*, trans. R. E. Carter (London, 1978) chap. XIX, §7, and Schoenberg, *Structural Functions of Harmony* (London, 1969) chaps. I and XI.
3 Boulez's comments are taken from the booklet accompanying his Deutsche Grammophon recording of *Parsifal* (DG 2713 004).
4 A. T. Katz, *Challenge to Musical Tradition. A New Concept of Tonality* (New York, 1945, repr. 1972) pp. 216–20.
5 F. Salzer, *Structural Hearing. Tonal Coherence in Music* (New York, 1952) vol. I, pp. 216–18. Salzer is clearly more liberal in his application of Schenker's basic techniques than Katz, but even he does not clarify the issue of how far a single tonal structure may extend.
6 As a type of seventh chord, this permeates the whole work. But its specific 'Tristan' form is especially clear at two other dramatically significant points in Act II: Parsifal's cry to the Flower Maidens, 'Lasst ab! Ihr fangt mich nicht!'; and later at Parsifal's 'nach der Verdammnis Quell zu schmachten!'.
7 R. P. Morgan, 'Dissonant Prolongation: Theoretical and Compositional Precedents', *Journal of Music Theory*, vol. XX, 1976, pp. 62–72.
8 For a recent discussion of Lorenz in the context of other analytical approaches to Wagner, see D. R. Murray, 'Major Analytical Approaches to Wagner's Musical Style: A Critique', *The Music Review*, vol. XXXIX, 1978, pp. 211–22.
9 I. Stravinsky, *An Autobiography* (New York, 1936) p. 38. Even so, Stravinsky apparently attended another performance of the work

fairly soon afterwards, in Monte Carlo on 26 January 1913 (see V. Stravinsky and R. Craft, *Stravinsky in Pictures and Documents* (London, 1979) p. 94).

10 In his *Debussy and Wagner* (London, 1979) Robin Holloway argues that 'Debussy must be recognized as the most profoundly Wagnerian of all composers' and that *'Parsifal* is the instrument of Debussy's achievement of his profoundest aims'. I find it hard to accept Holloway's analytical style, but his insights into both composers are valid and considerable.

4 Stage history

1   R. Wagner, *Gesammelte Schriften und Dichtungen,* vol. X, pp. 297–8.
2   C. Wagner, *Die Tagebücher,* vol. II, p. 181.
3   Quoted in *Wagner: A Documentary Study,* eds. H. Barth, D. Mack and E. Voss, trans. M. Whittall (London, 1975) p. 243.
4   C. Dahlhaus, 'Wagner', in *The New Grove Dictionary of Music and Musicians* (London, 1980).
5   A. Neumann, *Personal Recollections of Wagner,* trans. E. Livermore (London, 1909) p. 235.
6   *Ibid.* p. 250.
7   H. S. Chamberlain, *Richard Wagner,* trans. G. Ainslie Hight (London, 1900) p. 367.
8   R. Northcott, *Parsifal* (Illustrated Souvenir, London, 1914) p. 24.
9   Wieland Wagner to Karl Hermann, 1951, quoted in Bayreuth Festival programme *Parsifal,* 1973, p. 9.
10 Wieland Wagner to Hans Knappertsbusch, 1951, *ibid.* p. 7.
11 A. Appia, *La musique et la mise en scène* (Berne, 1963) p. 99 (this is the original French text of *Die Musik und die Inszenierung* of 1899).
12 W. Wagner to Hermann, quoted in Bayreuth Festival programme *Parsifal,* 1973, p. 9.
13 Appia, *La musique et la mise en scène,* p. 101.
14 W. Wagner, interview with C-H. Bachmann, 1964, quoted in Bayreuth Festival programme *Parsifal,* 1973, p. 37.
15 W. Wagner, interview with A. Golea, 1966, *ibid.* p. 46.
16 W. Wagner to W. Pitz, 1966, *ibid.* p. 47.
17 Quoted in G. Skelton, *Wieland Wagner: The Positive Sceptic* (London, 1971) p. 104.
18 W. Wagner, interview with Bachmann, quoted in Bayreuth Festival programme *Parsifal,* 1973, p. 42.
19 *Ibid.*
20 W. Wagner, interview with Golea, *ibid.* p. 46.

5 Reactions and critical assessments

1   Quoted in Erich Heller, *The Disinherited Mind* (Cambridge, 1952) p. 99.

2 Quoted in *Wagner: A Documentary Study*, eds. H. Barth *et al.*, p. 241.
3 E. Hanslick, *Music Criticisms 1846–99*, trans. Henry Pleasants (rev. edn, Harmondsworth, 1963) pp. 190, 194–6.
4 *Ibid.* pp. 204–5.
5 *Ibid.* p. 206
6 M. Kufferath, *Parsifal* (2nd edn, Paris, 1893) p. 213.
7 *Ibid.* p. 214.
8 E. Hippeau, *'Parsifal' et l'opéra wagnérien* (Paris, 1883) p. 38.
9 *Ibid.* p. 31.
10 G. Servières, *Richard Wagner jugé en France* (Paris, 1887), p. 250.
11 Kufferath, *Parsifal*, pp. 215–16.
12 *Ibid.* p. 221.
13 C. Debussy, *Monsieur Croche the Dilettante Hater* (anonymous trans., London, 1927) p. 111.
14 F. Hueffer, *Wagner's 'Parsifal'* (London, 1897) p. 10.
15 *Revue wagnérienne*, vol. I, 1885–6, p. 281.
16 *Revue wagnérienne*, vol. II, 1886–7, pp. 225–6.
17 *Revue wagnérienne*, vol. III, 1887–8, pp. 257–8.
18 Kufferath, *Parsifal*, pp. 222–3.
19 *Ibid.* pp. 174–7.
20 Quoted in C. von Westernhagen, *Wagner: A Biography*, trans. Mary Whittall (Cambridge, 1978) vol. II, p. 509.
21 *Ibid.* vol. II, pp. 534–5.
22 F. Nietzsche, *Nietzsche contra Wagner*, trans. Walter Kaufmann in *The Portable Nietzsche* (London, 1971) p. 676.
23 *Ibid.* pp. 674–5.
24 F. Nietzsche, *The Anti-Christ*, trans. R. J. Hollingdale (Harmondsworth, 1968) p. 186.
25 Quoted in J. P. Stern, *A Study of Nietzsche* (Cambridge, 1979) p. 15.
26 *Ibid.* p. 19.
27 *Ibid.* p. 23.
28 F. Nietzsche, *The Case of Wagner*, trans. T. Common in *The Works of F. Nietzsche* (London, 1899) vol. III, pp. 9–10.
29 *Ibid.* p. 13.
30 *Ibid.* p. 23.
31 *Ibid.* pp. 46–8.
32 *Ibid.* pp. 58–9.
33 T. Mann, *Essays of Three Decades*, trans. H. T. Lowe-Porter (London, 1947) pp. 329–30.
34 *Ibid.* pp. 336–7.
35 *Ibid.* pp. 402–3.
36 *Ibid.* pp. 409–10.
37 E. Newman, *Wagner as Man and Artist* (2nd edn, 1924, repr. London, 1963) pp. 374–6.
38 R. W. Gutman, *Richard Wagner* (London, 1968) pp. 422–3, 427, 428.
39 *Ibid.* pp. 431–2.

40 *Ibid.* p. 433.
41 *Ibid.* p. 439.
42 W. Diez, 'Prometheus, Lucifer and the Utopia of the Grail', in Bayreuth Festival programme *Parsifal,* 1972.
43 Wieland Wagner's *Parsifalkreuz* has often been reprinted, most accessibly in Skelton, *Wieland Wagner,* pp. 106–7, and in the booklet accompanying the 1970 Bayreuth recording of *Parsifal* conducted by Boulez (DG 2713 004).
44 See chap. 4, n. 20 above.
45 *Ibid.*
46 Dahlhaus, *Richard Wagner's Music Dramas,* pp. 143–4.
47 Dahlhaus, in book accompanying 1972 Decca recording of *Parsifal* conducted by Solti (Decca SET550–4), p. 2.
48 M. Tanner, 'The Total Work of Art', in *The Wagner Companion,* eds. P. Burbidge and R. Sutton (London, 1979) p. 208.
49 *Ibid.* p. 209.
50 *Ibid.* pp. 215–16.
51 *Ibid.* p. 218.

6 A proposed interpretation

 1 F. Liszt to Princess C. von Sayn-Wittgenstein, October 1872, quoted in R. Wagner, *Sämtliche Werke,* vol. XXX,p. 21.
 2 F. R. Leavis, *Lectures in America* (London, 1969) p. 54.
 3 J. Kerman, *Opera as Drama* (New York, 1956) p. 195.
 4 *Ibid.* pp. 213, 215.
 5 E. Heller, *The Disinherited Mind,* p. 62.
 6 R. Wagner, *My Life,* p. 662.
 7 *König Ludwig II und Richard Wagner Briefwechsel,* ed. O. Strobel (Karlsruhe, 1936–9) vol. I, p. 82.
 8 *Ibid.* vol. III, pp. 21–2.
 9 R. Wagner, *Gesammelte Schriften und Dichtungen* (Leipzig, 1883) vol. X, pp. 307–8.
10 From *Human, All Too Human,* 519, in R. J. Hollingdale, *Nietzsche* (London, 1973) p. 64.
11 From *The Will to Power,* 822, quoted in Hollingdale, *Nietzsche,* p. 155.
12 Heller, *The Disinherited Mind,* p. 126.
13 F. R. Leavis, *The Living Principle* (London, 1975) p. 248.
14 See chap. 5, n. 31.
15 F. Nietzsche, *Twilight of the Idols,* trans. R. J. Hollingdale (Harmondsworth, 1968) p. 72.
16 See *Arthurian Literature in the Middle Ages,* ed. R. S. Loomis (Oxford, 1959) pp. 230–4.
17 Leavis, *The Living Principle,* pp. 203, 245.
18 *Ibid.* p. 254.
19 *Ibid.* p. 236.
20 *Richard Wagner's Letters to August Röckel,* trans. E. C. Sellar (London, n.d.) p. 95.

21 2 Corinthians 5:18-21, *Jerusalem Bible* trans.
22 Quoted in E. Busch, *Karl Barth,* trans. J. Bowden (London, 1976) p. 100.
23 Heller, *The Disinherited Mind,* pp. 135–6.
24 As printed, with modernized spelling, in *The Faber Book of Religious Verse,* ed. H. Gardner (London, 1972) p. 67.

Bibliography

(There are references to *Parsifal* scattered everywhere in the vast Wagner literature. This short bibliography is divided into four categories: 1. Printed documents particularly rich in material on *Parsifal;* 2. Material on Wagner's principal source; 3. The best of the books entirely devoted to *Parsifal;* 4. Books containing exceptionally useful chapters or essays on *Parsifal.* Other references will be found in the notes to each chapter.)

1

Wagner, R. *Sämtliche Werke,* ed. C. Dahlhaus, vol. XXX, *Dokumente zur Entstehung und ersten Aufführung des Bühnenweihfestspiels Parsifal,* eds. M. Geck and E. Voss, Mainz, 1970

Wagner, R. Das Bühnenweihfestspiel in Bayreuth 1882 in *Gesammelte Schriften und Dichtungen,* Leipzig, 1883, vol. X; Eng. trans. in *Richard Wagner's Prose Works,* trans. W. Ashton Ellis, London, 1892–9, vol.

Wagner, R. *Richard Wagner an Mathilde Wesendonk: Tagebuchblätter und Briefe,* ed. W. Golther, Berlin 1904

Wagner, R. *König Ludwig II und Richard Wagner Briefwechsel,* 5 vols., ed. O. Strobel, Karlsruhe, 1936–9

Wagner, R. *Das braune Buch,* ed. J. Bergfeld, Zurich, 1975; Eng. trans. as *The Diary of Richard Wagner 1865-1882: The Brown Book,* by G. Bird, London, 1980

Wagner, Cosima, *Die Tagebücher,* 2 vols., eds. M. Gregor-Dellin and D. Mack, Munich, 1976–7; Eng. trans. of vol. I by G. Skelton, London, 1978

2

Wolfram von Eschenbach, *Parzival,* ed. K. Lachmann, 1833, rev. E. Hartl, 7th edn, Berlin, 1952; Eng. trans. by H. M. Mustard and C. E. Passage, New York, 1961; Modern German version used by Wagner: by K. Simrock, 1842; Commentary used by Wagner: San-Marte (A. Schulz), *Parzival-Studien,* 3 vols. 1861–2

For modern commentary on Wolfram and other medieval sources see: *Arthurian Literature in the Middle Ages,* ed. R. S. Loomis, Oxford, 1954

3

Chailley, J. *'Parsifal' de Richard Wagner: Opéra initiatique,* Paris, 1979
Golther, W. *Parsifal und der Gral in deutscher Sage des Mittelalters und der Neuzeit,* Leipzig, 1911
Hippeau, E. *'Parsifal' et l'opéra wagnérien,* Paris, 1883
Kufferath, M. *Parsifal,* 2nd edn, Paris, 1893

4

Dahlhaus, C. *Richard Wagners Musikdramen,* Velber, 1971; Eng. trans. by M. Whittall, Cambridge, 1979
Gutman, R. *Richard Wagner: The Man, His Mind and His Music,* London, 1968
Hanslick, E. *Music Criticisms 1846—99,* ed. and trans. H. Pleasants, rev. edn, London, 1963
Tanner, M. in *The Wagner Companion,* eds. P. Burbidge and R. Sutton, London, 1979
von Westernhagen, C. *Wagner,* Zurich, 1968; Eng. trans. by M. Whittall, Cambridge, 1978

Revue wagnérienne 3 vols. Paris, 1885—8, repr. 1971
Bayreuth Festival programme books on *Parsifal* 1951—79

Discography

BY MALCOLM WALKER

P	Parsifal	ⓜ	mono recording
Am	Amfortas	④	cassette version
T	Titurel	*	78 rpm disc
G	Gurnemanz	†	45 rpm disc
Kl	Klingsor	Ⓔ	electronically reprocessed
Kun	Kundry		stereo

all recordings are 33⅓ rpm in
stereo unless otherwise stated

1951   (live performances – Bayreuth Festival) Windgassen *P;* London *Am;* Van Mill *T;* Weber *G;* Uhde *Kl;* Mödl *Kun*/1951 Bayreuth Festival Chorus and Orch/Knappertsbusch
             Decca ⓜ GOM504–8
             Richmond ⓜ RS65001

1956   (live performance – Bayreuth Festival) Vinay *P;* Fischer-Dieskau *Am;* Greindl *T;* Hotter *G;* Neidlinger *Kl;* Mödl *Kun*/ 1956 Bayreuth Festival Chorus and Orch/Knappertsbusch
             Cetra ⓜ L079/5

1962   (live performance – Bayreuth Festival) Thomas *P;* London *Am;* Talvela *T;* Hotter *G;* Neidlinger *Kl;* Dalis *Kun*/1962 Bayreuth Festival Chorus and Orch/Knappertsbusch
             Philips 6747 250

1970   (live performances – Bayreuth Festival) King *P;* Stewart *Am;* Ridderbusch *T;* Crass *G;* McIntyre *Kl;* G. Jones *Kun*/1970 Bayreuth Festival Chorus and Orch/Boulez
             DG 2713 004

1972   Kollo *P;* Fischer-Dieskau *Am;* Hotter *T;* Frick *G;* Kelemen *Kl;* Ludwig *Kun*/Vienna Boys' Choir, Vienna State Opera Chorus, VPO/Solti   Decca SET550–4 ④ K113K54
             London OSA1510

1975   (live performance ⓝ Leipzig Congress Hall) Kollo *P;* Adam *Am;* Tescher *T;* Cold *G;* Bunger *Kl;* Schroter *Kun*/Berlin Radio Choir, Leipzig Radio Choir, St Thomas's Church Choir, Leipzig Radio SO/Kegel

             Eterna 827031-5

1925   (excerpts – in English) Widdop *P;* Heming *Am;* Radford *G;*

158

Baker *Kl;* Ljungberg *Kun* /chorus and orch/A. Coates
HMV D1025−31, DB862*

1928   (Act 3) Pistor *P;* Bronsgeest *Am;* Hofmann *G*/Berlin State
Opera Chorus and Orch/Muck
Preiser ⓜ LV100

1950s   (excerpts) Neumeyer *P;* Meesen *Kun;* Ramms *G*/Dresden State
Opera Orch/Schreiber   Allegro ⓜ ALL3095

1927   (Acts 1 and 2 − excerpts) Bayreuth Festival Chorus and Orch/
Muck & S. Wagner   Columbia L2007−14*
Am. Columbia set M337*

1943   (Act 1 Prelude; Act 3) Hartmann *P;* Reinmar *Am;* Weber *G;*
Larcen *Kun;*/German Opera House Chorus and Orch., Berlin/
Knappertsbusch
Acanta ⓜ DE23036

Prelude and Good Friday Music
NBC SO/Toscanini   RCA (US) ⓜ VIC1278
RCA (UK) ⓜ VCM5

Berlin PO/Furtwängler   EMI ⓜ 1C 147 29229−30
Seraphim ⓜ IB6024

Bavarian Radio SO/Jochum   DG 2548 221
Concertgebouw/Haitink   Philips 6500 932 ④ 7300 391

Prelude
Philharmonia/Klemperer   EMI SLS5075 ④ TC−SLS5075

Preludes: Acts 1 and 3 − excerpts
LPO/Boult   EMI ASD3000
Angel S37090

Act 1
Titurel, der fromme Held
Greindl/Württemberg State Orch/Leitner
DG ⓜ EPL32045†
Amfortas's lament − Nein! Lasst ihn unenthüllt!
Edelmann/VSO/Moralt   Philips ⓜ ABR4030
Schoeffler/Vienna State Opera Orch/Prohaska
Saga Ⓔ 5290
Fischer-Dieskau/Bavarian Radio SO/Kubelik
HMV ASD3499
Angel S37487Q

Act 2
Kundry/Parsifal duet − Dies alles hab' ich nun geträumt?
Flagstad, Melchior/RCA Victor Orch/McArthur
RCA (US) ⓜ VIC1681
RCA (UK) ⓜ VCM5
Nilsson, Brilioth/Royal Opera House Orch, Covent Garden/Segerstam
Philips 6500 661

Ich sah' das kind
Leider/LSO/Barbirolli   EMI   Ⓜ   1C 147 30785–6M
Traubel/RCA Victor Orch/Weissmann   EMI   Ⓜ   7ER5027†
Varnay/Philharmonia/Weigert   EMI   Ⓜ   1C 047 01373M

Act 3
Good Friday scene (Parsifal/Gurnemanz)
Ralf, Weber/VPO/Moralt   EMI LX1394*
Gurnemanz's part *only*
Greindl/Wurttemberg State Orch/Leitner
                        DG   Ⓜ   2721 115

Orchestral only version
RPO/Beecham   Philips   Ⓜ   GL5635
                        CBS (US)   Ⓜ   ML4962

Amfortas's lament – Ja! Wehe! Wehe!
Fischer-Dieskau/Bavarian Radio SO/Kubelik
                        EMI ASD3499
                        Angel S37487Q

Nur eine Waffe taugt
Melchior/Danish State Radio SO/Malko
                        DG   Ⓜ   2721 109
Ralf/Metropolitan Opera Orch/Busch
                        CBS 71824D*

Index